FOR ENID WITH LOVE
a festschrift

FOR ENID WITH LOVE
a festschrift

A Collection of Essays, Poems, and
Reminiscences for Enid Dame

Edited by Barry Wallenstein

The New York Quarterly Foundation, Inc.
New York, New York

NYQ Books™ is an imprint of The New York Quarterly Foundation, Inc.

The New York Quarterly Foundation, Inc.
P. O. Box 2015
Old Chelsea Station
New York, NY 10113

www.nyqbooks.org

First Edition

Set in New Baskerville

Layout by Raymond P. Hammond
Cover Design by Natalie Sousa
Cover Photo by Layle Silbert

Library of Congress Control Number: 2010936317

ISBN: 978-1-935520-12-2

FOR ENID WITH LOVE
a festschrift

Contents

Preface by Barry Wallenstein / ix

Introduction by Donald Lev / 13
  "Some Thoughts on the Life and Work of Enid Dame"

1. Laurence Carr—"Hearing Enid Dame" / 26
2. Patricia Eakins—"Enid Dame and Her Grip on God" / 28
3. Phillis Gershator—"Who's Not Ready, Holler I:
    A Review of an Unpublished Novel by Enid Dame" / 31
4. Dimitri Kalantzis—"The Queen of Brighton Beach" / 34
5. Burt Kimmelman—"Enid Dame's Householdry" / 37
6. Careufel de Lamière—"Remembering Enid" / 50
7. Linda Lerner—"On Enid Dame" / 52
8. Patricia Markert—"Enid Dame's Voice" / 55
9. D. H. Melhem—"Enid Dame's Legacy, from Enid
    Dame Tribute, March 21, 2004, CedarTavern" / 59
10. Alicia Ostriker—"Enid Dame: Midrashic Prophet" / 63
11. Judith P. Saunders—"Enid Dame and the Hudson
    River Valley" / 70
12. Two brief testimonies:
    Susan Sindall and Harry Smith / 76
13. Maxine Susman—"Enid: In Remembrance" / 77
14. Karen Swenson—a brief testimony / 83
15. Madeline Tiger—"Bless This Garden, A Review of
    Stone Shekhina, Poems by Enid Dame" / 84
16. Martin Tucker—"There Is Nothing Like an
    Enid Dame" / 94

Appendix 1: A Selection of Enid's Poems

"Chagall Exhibit, 1996" / 99
"Mike Gold and the Classics" / 101
"Lilith, I Don't Cut My Grass" / 103
"The Woman Who Was Water" / 105

Appendix 2: A Selection of Poems to Enid

"Russian Snow in Brooklyn" by David Gershator / 109
"Poetry Teacher" by Roberta Gould / 111
"Bat Mitzvah—Portion Noah" by Walter Hess / 112
"A Little Something—for Enid" by Bob Holman / 114
"Enid" by Judith Lechner / 115
"Poem for Enid Dame" by Ellen Aug Lytle / 116
"Epithalamion for Enid and Don" by D. H. Melhem / 117
"You Enid Dame With Your Cloud of Beautiful Hair
    and your Kindness" by Constance Norgren / 118
"For Enid Dame" by Ed Sanders / 120
"A Cup for Enid" by Cheryl A. Rice / 122
"Lilith Mourns" by Matthew J. Spireng / 123
"For Enid Dame, Poet" by Nikki Stiller / 124
"Enid Dame" by Yerra Sugarman / 127
"Sestinas of the City 'Cluttered with Roses'"
    by Madeline Tiger / 129
"Enid" by Janine Pommy Vega / 131
"Sparkle Like Diamonds, A Review"
    by Carletta Joy Walker / 133
"Without Tears for Enid" by Barry Wallenstein / 136

Appendix 3: Two Essays by Enid Dame

"'I May Be a Bit of a Jew': What Contemporary Jewish American Poets Learned from Allen Ginsberg and Sylvia Plath" / 139

"Art as Midrash: Some Notes on the Way to a Discussion" / 150

Appendix 4: Selected List of Enid's Publications

An Enid Dame Bibliography / 163

Contributor Notes / 165

Acknowledgments / 177

Preface

by Barry Wallenstein

This is not the first gathering of songs of love and admiration dedicated to Enid Dame. A year after she died in 2003, poems, tribute essays, and personal memories appeared throughout the 2004 [# 50], issue of *Home Planet News,* the journal she founded and edited along with her life's partner and husband, Donald Lev. This new collection, *For Enid with Love,* was conceived in 2007 by Donald Lev with the assistance of the poet D. H. Melhem. Herein are essays of personal remembrance, individual appreciations of her artistry, poems written in her memory, and some written especially for the occasion of this book. A good number of these pieces were written by people who never met Enid but were moved by her art and the story of her life.

This is actually a *festschrift,* a festival of writings, which the dictionary defines as a "volume for presentation to a well-known scholar on the occasion of her attaining a certain age, pinnacle of her career, retirement." Enid achieved her pinnacle and retired too soon. Although she did teach, and some of the testimony here is by colleagues who praise her teaching, she was other than a "well-known scholar." But as she was a student and poet of *midrash,* she lived her scholarship and made the most moving, most humane art out of her deeply felt learning. While collecting the materials for this tribute book, it has been supremely rewarding to get to know better this writer, poet, and teacher.

I met Enid when she was a student at CCNY and attending one of the early Annual Spring Poetry Festivals. Enid read her poems at this event and returned each spring to participate—as did (and does) Donald. Her inimitable voice and warm-spirited humor radiated in her poems and her life.

This feeling of being moved by her presence and delightfully informed by her life's work, is revisited and revealed in each of the contributions here. The cumulative effect of this gathering of encomiums should bring Enid back alive as only language and art can do.

In many ways, her poetry is about the life cycle, including of course endings. Midway in her first book *Between Revolutions* (1977), the poem "Trouble with Endings" begins: "I have/ trouble with endings./ Remember the time/ we fought about/ the working class?" Well, Enid was fiercely engaged all the way through, as an artist and as a political activist, and she struggled against the terrible reality, prefigured in this poem near its close—"The ending/ we weren't prepared for/ swallows us whole." The poem closes with a rhetorical question, "What will we become/ in the ocean's belly?" All the thoughts, observations, and feelings present in this collection attest to what Enid Dame has become—a living presence in lives of those who discover her work, as much as in the minds and hearts of those who knew her. Alicia Ostriker, who expresses this thought best in the conclusion of her essay, "Enid Dame: Midrashic Prophet":

> *Her midrashic writing is a tree of life sprouting through disasters. Her writing as a whole is sharply political without being simple-minded, passionate and humane without sacrificing playfulness. May her work continue to ripple out her lefty spirit of truth and compassion and comedy and justice and life. May it live and be healthy.*

FOR ENID WITH LOVE
a festschrift

Some Thoughts on the Life and Work of Enid Dame
by Donald Lev

I first met Enid (who was my companion, wife, and colleague for 25 years) through some poems she sent to the New York Poets' Cooperative in 1976. The Co-op started in '69 as an organization that promoted readings—at that period you couldn't get more than five minutes anywhere in NYC to present your work orally unless you kissed ass at one of two holy edifices—St. Marks in the Bowery or the 92nd Street Y. I thought, what is this? Who is this? Does she really spell her last name with an m not an n? Does she either not know what she's doing or does the sober but funny magic of those unusual poems come from a genuine ability and authority? I guessed the latter and voted with the majority (I believe it was unanimous) to welcome her into membership. One of the poems, "Before," which subsequently appeared in her first Downtown Poets' chapbook *Between Revolutions* began:

> The catshit reproaches me in the bathroom.
> The icebox has regressed:
> incontinent, it leaks
> and puddles on the floor.
> The drain's in pain again.
> It vomits when I do the dishes.
> The dishes crack.
>
> We're all of us
> a bit unwell.

I finally got to meet Enid Dame at a meeting of the New York Poets' Cooperative. And I came to appreciate her cool literary and political intelligence as well as her inner warmth, honesty, and humor. We soon became friends. When, in 1978, Mike Devlin and I were beginning to produce issues of *Poets Monthly* out of Mike's strategic office in Union Square, I suggested to Mike that we needed a good, organized, literary-minded person to center the enterprise. He agreed. So I got

Enid, who at that time was looking for an excuse to lay off her doctoral dissertation for a while (she eventually finished it and became a fully exploitable member of Academia) to take on the task with the title of "associate editor." But before that time Enid and I met in connection with two other interesting New York City literary institutions of the time: The Print Center and the Downtown Poets' Cooperative.

The Print Center, in Brooklyn, was where all the small press publishers went in the '70s and '80s to put their chapbooks and other publications together. Any work you could do yourself, say saddle stitching, trimming, or even typesetting on one of their fine IBM Composers, you did yourself, without any cost to you. And anything the Print Center did for you—which was printing for the most part—was done at very reasonable rates—thanks to NYSCA and NEA funding. The operation was run by poets. Among the many many small presses that enjoyed the benefits of the Print Center was the Downtown Poets' Coop. headed by David and Phillis Gershator, two excellent writers and poets themselves, who managed on grants, which were much more plentiful those days, to publish several books and chapbooks. The *Downtown* authors whose names are most recognizable today were Ivan Arguelles, Irving Stettner, and Enid Dame.

Enid's two Downtown Poets' chapbooks, *Between Revolutions* (named "one of the half dozen best of the year" in 1977 by Bill Katz of the *Library Journal*) and *Interesting Times* (1978), both well printed and illustrated with interesting collages and photographs by her husband of the time, Robin Dame (who, changed in name and gender, is still a good friend and important member of the *Home Planet News* editorial staff), consists of poems reflecting a period of Enid's life when she was coming off a long hiatus during which poetry had been replaced by politics (she was a member of that section of SDS which did not use drugs or play with bombs, but also did not get to write the histories of the movement). Now, having left the party which denounced her as a "Bourgeois Individualist" and moved with husband and cats to Brooklyn, she began writing the funny, sad, nostalgic poems that appear in these books—all soaked in a marinade of place, politics, and Jewish ethnicity.

> four days a week
> I manage
> the streets, the terrible subways
> the human explosions
> skirting disasters
> between revolutions
> food cats poetry
> sex keep me sane
>
> the recent past
> almost sustains me:
> Browning and Ruskin
> Victorian novels
>
> energy
> hoarded and measured
> an inch at a time
>
> my friends
> know the score:
> "politics
> are meaningless,
> the past a bad joke…"
>   …
> yet
> history rumbles
> under the surface
>
> the sea
> caught in a conch shell

(from Between Revolutions)

Today
Brooklyn looks like Russia
In the snow.
The subway stop:
snow on its roof
snow down the tracks
like a railroad station
after a revolution.
People stand muffled:
boots woolen mittens furs
and shopping bags. A woman
reads a Yiddish paper.
A man reads *The Daily World.*

   ...

We huddle
like survivors...

("Waiting" in *Interesting Times*)

Place, politics, Jewish ethnicity continued to bathe Enid Dame's poetry whatever the genre, the theme, the form. What she called Midrashic poetry—poems concerned with biblical characters and stories with a view to fill in the blank spaces and answer questions raised in the scriptural narratives—was to become her primary concern, filling the whole of two of her subsequent collections, and major parts of the other three. Poems about family, poems about political protest, poems about her beloved Brooklyn (a new anthology, *Broken Land,* has recently emerged from NYU Press dedicated to Enid), and poems about personages from history and from the arts—Ethel Rosenberg, Marc Chagall, Sylvia Plath, Mike Gold—are present in abundance. The sestina and the villanelle are the formal resources she occasionally and with notable skill had recourse to. And the dramatic monologue (a Victorian scholar, she was a great admirer of Browning) is her special forte. Here are lines from her signature poem, "Lilith":

16

Kicked myself out of paradise
left a hole in the morning
no note   no goodbye

the man I lived with
was patient and hairy

he cared for the animals
worked late at night
planting vegetables
under the moon...

Taking hints from a 1972 article by Lilly Rivlin in *Ms* and
Susan Sherman's poem "Lilith of the Wildwood, of the Fair
Places," which was first printed in 1971 (both pieces are re-
printed in *Which Lilith? Feminist Writers Re-Create the World's
First Woman* (Jason Aronson, 1998), an anthology edited by
Enid Dame, Lilly Rivlin, and Henny Wenkart), Enid convert-
ed Lilith from the Judaeo-Christian Demon to a perennial
hip Jewish feminist with some sisterly connections to Mae
West and Sadie Thompson.

the middle ages
were sort of fun
they called me a witch
I kept dropping
in and out
of people's sexual fantasies

A delightful transitional poem appeared in Enid's chapbook,
Interesting Times. This is "Vildeh Chaya" which she pointed out
in her article "Art as Midrash" (published posthumously in
Home Planet News #53) was "(a) pivotal poem for me...(n)ot
exactly a midrash since there is no such character as Vildeh
Chaya in Jewish text. I invented her—a wild Jewish woman—
because of a misunderstanding on the part of my mother
(who) thought this Yiddish expression actually referred to an
archetypal shtetl character—wild Chaya."

17

Vildeh Chaya
in the woods   on the edge
of the shtetl   she hides
mud-splattered   dress torn
barefoot   she won't
peel potatoes   get married
cut her hair off   have children
keep the milk dishes
separate
from the meat dishes

instead, she
climbs trees   talks to animals
naked   sings half-crazy
songs to the moon. ...

(*Interesting Times* p.26)

Poems in *Anything You Don't See* (West End Press, 1992), her
most comprehensive volume, catalogue Enid's family history
from her birth in Beaver Falls, a small mill town in western
Pennsylvania

The walls shook, and I broke into the world,
skidded into a bedrail and found my voice
in the summer hospital room, in the quiet milltown.
Mother shuddered, "I think it's already happened."
"Impossible!" Father insisted. "It's still too early."
The doctor, meanwhile, was out fishing. ...

("Birthday")

to politically progressive parents who met at a labor rally in
Washington, D.C. when they were young government work-
ers during the New Deal 'thirties who suddenly removed to
Pennsylvania where her father (originally from The Bronx)
became a furniture salesman (introduced into that calling by

his father-in-law); to the city of Pittsburgh, where Enid spent her early teens, and her Indiana-born mother—who suffered from depression, and, later, from multiple sclerosis—painted.

> In Mother's city, there are no doorknobs.
> Someone has pulled up the trees.
> In this Pittsburgh, the sky is yellow,
> oilspilled, streaky. The color of despair.
> Telephone poles throw up hands,
> gawky crosses, then fall over backward.
> No wires. No birds. Here,
> everything is inside.
>
> ("Mother's City")

In Pittsburgh Enid started high school—which had a writer's club. Then the family (which by now also included her younger brother Phil Jacobs—currently editor of the *Baltimore Jewish Times*) moved to Baltimore where there was no writer's club. So Enid joined the gun club. Thence to Towson State Teacher's College (now University) where she published poems in the *Talisman* (Towson's literary magazine), got involved with the science fiction "fanzine" movement, where she met her first husband, married, got involved with the Baltimore peace movement, graduated, taught high school; then dumped it all, "caught the red-eye to New York/ reading 'America' in the City Lights Edition,/ ecstatic on no sleep and bursts of fantasy..." ("The Seders", published in the *Woodstock Journal*).

The borough Enid loved so passionately is celebrated even more strongly than in the previous volumes in *Anything You Don't See*. Consider such classics as "Brighton Beach" ("...a place of immigrants, radicals, exiles,/ serious eaters and various gifts...") and "Riding the D-Train":

> Notice the rooftops,
> the wormeaten Brooklyn buildings.

Houses crawl by,
each with its private legend.
In one, a mother
is punishing her child
slowly, with great enjoyment.
In one, a daughter
is writing a novel
she can't show to anyone. ...

In this volume also, her powerful sestinas begin to appear:
"My Father and the Brooklyn Bridge," "Sestina for Michael,"
and "Ethel Rosenberg: A Sestina":

I picture you in your three-room apartment, a
     woman
singing snatches of arias to yourself as you set the
     table,
loving and hating the house. I know the type.
Scraping and rearranging, refusing to take things
     easy,
foreboding washes over you, an extra sense.

Dramatic monologues are here in abundance. Besides the
midrashic Lot and Eve, we are addressed in the voices of Cin-
derella, Persephone, and citizens of Brighton Beach like the
persona of "Closing Down: Old Woman on Boardwalk":

Still holding on in this body,
an old house;
one by one they're sealing its rooms off.
Heat's disappearing
like ghosts through the cracks.

In the last section of the book, Enid celebrates her parents'
lives and deaths in several haunting poems.

Now   hold your mother
lingeringly on your tongue.

20

Her fruit is still alive.
It tastes as it always did:
heavy resonant edgy.
It makes you think of old coats
fur collared camphor-scented
worn in another country.

("Fruit Cellar"}

Inside my father's blood
a battle is raging,
directed by doctors and chemical companies.
He's been invaded twice.
Like any other war,
this one is heavy with talk
of blasting, destruction, intrigues,
and, naturally, false reports.

("What We're Here For")

In the elegant "God's Lioness," also in *Anything You Don't See,*
Enid Dame addresses one of her great models, Sylvia Plath:

Art can do just so much—
it can't save you.

These lines move me to reflect on Enid Dame's late poems,
haunted by cancer, 9/11, and impending war. This from an
unpublished poem, "Bulbs":

You gave me six daffodil bulbs
to plant in my upstate front yard,
letting each one stand for an unrescued name
entombed in the Tower wreckage.

I carried the box to my mountain,
set to work with a shovel.
It proved slow going,
that ungiving October day.

21

One of the bulbs had split:
two bodies joined at the stem.
I thought of those mythic co-workers
who held hands before they jumped.
...
I thought: I'm burying six people
I probably never knew,
their bodies unfound   their names amputated.
All we'll have is six flowers

if they actually bloom next spring,
if we're here to see, to remember.

Those daffodils have been blooming ever since, more profusely each spring. The theme of remembering became important in these last (perhaps Anthroposophy-influenced) poems. In "Catskill Mountain Book Fair: May 2003" (published in *Heliotrope*) she begins:

Remember it all.
It won't be here next year.

Woman poet in red velvet blouse on stage.
Grand piano (covered like a toaster) behind her.
Pieces of quilt on the walls.
Publishers listening at their booths.
Backdrop: a road climbing a mountain,
trees slowly finding their green,
an apple tree in frail flower.

One poem lays cold fingers
on your shoulders.
You shudder in ecstasy.
The next poet reads too much.
Everyone here is good-humored.
Remember them all.

You reach for a hand.
It is here this year.
It feels warm and comfortable. You handle it
while the poems' rhythms gently rock the room.
This is a pleasure. You will need
to remember it later. ...

In emulation of another great role model, especially during
the last year of her life, the Mexican painter and political
activist Frieda Kahlo, Enid participated in peace demonstra-
tions and recorded what it felt like to be in those moments
in poems like her villanelle, "The War Moves Closer," printed
posthumously in both *Home Planet News* and the "Beat Bush"
issue of *Long Shot*:

> The war moves closer and we can't stop it.
> Four million marched in Rome and London.
> We read our poems on a Woodstock stage.
> Winter goes on forever.
>
> Four million marched in Rome and London.
> A few lay down in the snow in Antarctica.
> Winter goes on forever. ...

and the monumental "This One," also published posthu-
mously, in *Tikkun*:

> The first one wasn't real.
> But I opposed it.
> I opposed it in a workshirt.
> I opposed it in a mini-skirt.
> I opposed it on my way to buy birth-control pills.
> I oppposed it ecstatically.
> I opposed it in my kitchen bathtub
> on the Lower East Side.
> I opposed it on the streets with my friends
> who were scruffy and raucous and funny,
> who opposed it with their youth and great bodies.

...
This one is different.
We've lost so much already:
a city
a democracy
a way to be together
a fantasy of hope
(which glimmered like a silver-misted island
at the edge of possibility).

Now it's hard to see that island
through the thickening smoke.

An awful force is gathering.
It's real. It's getting stronger.
It doesn't mean us well.

But I'll oppose it
with my smoke-clogged brain.
I'll oppose it with a stone in my breast...

On December 3, 2003, during a bitter, unseasonable, cold spell, Enid flew out to Ann Arbor, Michigan, to read at a fundraiser for the Jewish feminist journal *Bridges,* of which she had been a poetry editor. She died of pneumonia and complications from breast cancer three weeks later, on Christmas day.

I'm going to conclude here. Not that there isn't more to say. This has been little more than a brisk survey covering the small part of Enid Dame's work included in the seven books and chapbooks published during her lifetime. I have said nothing of her fiction, or of her editorial work on three periodicals and an important anthology; nor have I spoken much of her scholarship, which included writings on Victorian literature, Jewish-American fiction, and of course midrashic poetry and Jewish feminism. Besides her work on *Which Lilith?* noted above, she wrote papers, gave lectures and presentations of her own and other women's work, and at the time of her death was working on a second anthology, this one of writings on the Prophetess Miriam. This project has reached some fruition in a recent issue of *Bridges*.

Hundreds of notebooks attest to Enid's serious life-long reflections on, and struggles with, poetry, teaching (which she took very seriously), politics, history, Jewish-American literature and religion, and, finally, cancer, and the meaning of life. This little essay is meant to break some ice over deep, deep water.

1. Hearing Enid Dame

by Laurence Carr

It was at the old Bohemian Book Bin, a room surrounded by books from the cop-thriller to the "how-to," from Austen to Zoroaster. A listening room of musings; we lull in the arms of Kalliope and her friends.

Poet and champion of local writers, Teresa Costa, was hosting a featured reading along with an open mic. It was one of the many gatherings of wordsmiths and their tribe that echoed throughout the Hudson Valley on any given night throughout the year, cancelled only by sleety hail or bitter storm and sometimes not even then.

An older gentleman approached the bench, disheveled as a poet is, outwardly, but with a well so deep, one knew there were currents of waterwords yet to be plumbed. I was laying eyes on Donald Lev, now at last matching name and face. He spoke in that Damon Runyon voice that carried me to another place and time, to a basement coffeehouse, filled with smoke and snap. He read from himself and of himself and then he paused.

"I want to read a poem by Enid Dame." No more than that. It was all that was needed for introduction, testament and the poet's solemn plea for the world to stop for one brief moment.

He read her poem, "Untenanted."

> Standing over
> Your uninhabited body,
> Father,
> I kept thinking,
> "The building is still there."

And as he read, I began my own journey, to fathers here and

fathers gone, to father's fathers and fathers yet to come. And as he read, I sensed Enid Dame among us. Is this why he reads her, to bring her back, or to bring us comfort in the fact that she has never left?

> …warm,
> a brick wall
> still holding in the sun.

The arc was completed, the pathway laid. From here to here. She leads the way. She had to go first, to keep the rest of us from being lost.

2. Enid Dame and Her Grip on God

by Patricia Eakins

E.e. cummings said, "always the beautiful answer who asks a more beautiful question."

What particularly spoke to me in Enid's poetry was her on-going dialogue with religious tradition and scriptures, her midrash. She certainly did not see the old teachings as irrelevant or outmoded; she engaged in a dialogue of re-interpretation that was both sharply challenging and richly affirming. In "Miriam's Seders," for instance she questions the four questions that are at the heart of the ritual, questions which are traditionally asked of the four sons—the smart one, the rebellious one, the simple one, the innocent one. Painfully aware that women—daughters—simply do not enter this picture, she re-casts the four sons as four daughters, asserting that "we [humans] are all the four sons," refusing an easy anger that would reject tradition and leave her isolated from its consolations. Her readings of stories about Sarah and Hagar, Eve and Lilith, Noah and his family, are a rich dance of humor, anger, identification, and empathy, as she struggles to make them relevant and contemporary and to separate timeless wisdom from time-bound prejudice and convention. There is nothing abstract or intellectual about her involvement. She sucks the stories for meaning like fruits for juice, savoring each drop. She acknowledges that Judaism is a difficult religion for women, who must find a full place in it against resistance. Yet her struggle with that resistance comes to seem like the very wrestling of Jacob with the angel of the lord. As Enid might have said, we are all Jacob, fighing for our place in the story. By the tenacity of her grip on the angel, she demonstrates her worth as a claimant. She will not let go of God; the strength of her grip shows that God will not let go of her. This was Enid's striking contribution to both feminism and religion—a contribution that only a poet and storyteller could make.

Enid did not engage in midrash with the teachings and text of the so-called "New Testament," or with the body of related doctrine and tradition. She did not need to find a way to relate to Christianity. Yet she showed me how I might engage in midrash with these teachings, doctrines, and traditions. And that seems very important to me, for there is much in Christianity that I find difficult. The doctrine of Immaculate Conception, among others. The Episcopal Bishop of San Francisco has said that he has no patience with anyone who worries overmuch about this doctrinal point. Look at the icon, he says. You see a mother and a baby. How do you react to that mother, that baby? His direct cutting through is quite reductive next to the complicated dance in which Enid might have engaged, a dance in which I imagine she would have woven a looping complicated story. Enid would never have dismissed any question. She would never have looked at that mother, that baby, without seeing another woman, a woman without a baby, a harlot, a woman not loved of God, a woman not most blessed but most cursed, a woman, perhaps, whose baby was born of rape by enemy soldiers or "cleansing" by male relatives after a husband's death. For Enid, nothing was ever simple, no story ever linear, not even—most especially not even—the story of God and the people of God. How can we see God's love in the vulnerability of women to sexual ravage? How can we relate the old story of virgin birth to the world of today, seen unflinchingly? Never one to duck a tricky question or a difficult assignment, Enid gives me courage to wrestle with a question the good bishop would have urged me to drop, yet her aim is very much the same as his: to find a way to relate to the stories that have been claimed in the literalist readings of rigid fundamentalists.

These fundamentalists often seem to "own" Christianity, to the point where a lefty like me can feel embarrassed to claim that she is a "Christian." Because "they" own that word, as they own "patriotic." In her bold, gay, assertive manner, Enid spoke back to the rigid traditionalists within Judaism, and by her example pointed a way for me to speak back to the rigid traditionalists within Christianity. When I look at the power that conservative Christianity is exerting in the life of our nation, I can think of no more important work for me to do as a storyteller and poet, as a spiritual person, or as a political person. And Enid as much as any other writer I have known pointed the way, not only with her work on the page, but with her remarkable presence as a reader of her own poems, the sheer pleasure she took in them, the richness of her speaking voice, shot through with tears and with laughter, with the full range and force of her personality and her potentiality. She was so fully who she was! How can we not be as fully who we are?

This was the challenge Enid laid down, in her gentle, yet audacious manner. There is much midrash left to write.

3. *Who's Not Ready, Holler I:* a review of an unpublished novel by Enid Dame

by Phillis Gershator

When Enid Dame asked me if I wanted to read her novel-in-progress, *Who's Not Ready, Holler I*, I jumped at the chance. I was impressed with it, thought it eminently publishable, and offered, when she was ready, to send it to a couple of editors I thought would be interested.

We'd occasionally talk about the novel. Once in a while Enid told me about feedback she'd gotten from workshops. Over time, she published excerpts of *Who's Not Ready* in various journals. One short story in *Confrontation* (Long Island University, Nos. 30-31, November 1985), "I Know a Good One," features almost the same characters as the family in *Who's Not Ready*. It's a fulfilling, layered story, a perfect example of Enid's voice: understated, wry, touching, and deeper than initially meets the eye, even when it comes to the final closing sentence.

When I did send the manuscript for *Who's Not Ready* out for review, the word that came back was that the "historical period," with its references to red diaper babies and Sixties' political activism, was not of current interest: "The Sixties are dead." Since then, we've seen books coming out on that same period, and on red diaper babies, too, which proves those editors wrong, wrong in more ways than one. Though its characters do debate ideas and ideology, *Who's Not Ready* is more than a political novel. It's a novel of family and of personal evolution. It's also, simply, a good read, visual and visceral enough to make me think Movie!

Enid Dame writes with hidden artfulness, never showy or flashy, no matter how fresh the metaphors and similes. She's solid, wise, and observant, with a down to earth, nuanced simplicity that recalls the fiction of Anne Tyler. Maybe there's something about Baltimore that inspires this seemingly effortless style: sympathetic, flawed, complicated characters; realistic dialogue; perfect pitch. The major difference is that Enid's fiction, from what I know about her life, contains many more autobiographical elements, and her domestic drama speaks directly to the concept of the "personal is political."

Her novel casts a wide net, interweaving themes such as terminal cancer, sibling rivalry, marital discord, infidelity, and political activism. In every incident and vignette, she explores the intersection of ideology, behavior, choice, and social pressure, and she does it with humor, pathos, and honesty. Her themes play out in an intense, condensed saga of 20th century life, beginning with a history familiar to many left wing Jewish families. A family moves out into the wider world to experience the awkwardness, on the one hand, of being a Jew in a Gentile environment or, on the other, a secular Jew in an Orthodox environment. Nothing is black and white; shades of gray abound; and in the post-war anti-communist world, so does secrecy, prejudice—and fear.

The Sixties mark a new, fearless beginning. In one flashback, Clara, the novel's main protagonist, remembers: "Now they are running together, they are leaping over barricades, they are dancing in the air. The demonstration has become a party, a carnival. Nothing can happen to them because they are right, and their enemies are wrong, and anyway the police and their horses are not real, they're keystone cops, hobbyhorses, cartoon figures; only they are real because they know anything is possible, they can make anything happen." But when a decade or two goes by, and Clara sees a tie-dyed T-shirt, she thinks: "Sixties nostalgia. Oh no, we've become camp."

It's Clara's nature throughout the novel to question: What were her parents' beliefs? Where does she fit in? Clara questions a poster of Woodstock as symbolic of the Sixties, just as she questions a Rosie the Riveter poster as symbolic of the

Forties. Historical moments, like life, are too complex, too contradictory to be summed up with an image, a moral, a happy ending.

People are real in this novel—they are jealous, pretentious, idealistic, secretive, optimistic, romantic, competitive, curious, angry, sexy, obsessed, dissatisfied, flirtatious, manipulative, resilient…. Relationships are rocky. Death is around the corner. But hope survives, and small things, as opposed to abstractions and ideology, make a difference. Food makes a difference. Love makes a difference. Saving a community garden in the Bronx makes a difference….

Who's Not Ready, Holler I is more than a window into Enid Dame's chronological life; it's imaginative fiction, after all, not autobiography. But her own interests and humanistic values clearly shine through, and her voice is her own distinctive voice: warm, witty, passionate, and above all, honest.

4. The Queen of Brighton Beach
by Dimitri Kalantzis

It feels impossible to describe life in New York City to the non-native; even harder to describe what it was like growing up in Brooklyn. Even Manhattanites appear unaware that those in the outer boroughs refer to Manhattan as "the City," a place you go to with a distinct purpose: a specialty store, an immigration lawyer, or a Broadway show. But in recent years I've heard of the growing celebrity of my hometown. Brooklyn, it seems, is making a comeback. Brooklyn, it seems, is recovering her glass slipper having lost it sometime long ago in some after hours bar in Sheepshead Bay. But what Prince is delivering it back? And what would the Queen of Brighton Beach, Enid Dame, say if she were still riding the D-train to the fish-mongering streets of Little Odessa?

I think she would find it all amusing. I think she would giggle and maybe even redden at the thought that the *New York Times* (in South Brooklyn the fourth option *at best* after the *Post* and *News*, and lowly *Newsday*) is reporting Brooklyn not for its vagrants but fashionistas, not for Coney Island alone, but posh little cafes you need a credit card to eat in. And she'd probably say in her squeakyvoice, I remember when it was the D-train that you took down through Brooklyn and the Q was only the Express. But then again she'd probably say she wasn't surprised at all by the changes. After all, Brooklyn, a city unto itself, spent the better part of the 20th century just catching up to its inhabitants. No more socialists (real ones at least) and no more Ebbets Field; we have Troubadour Russian punks and the Brooklyn Cyclones. Whether or not she'd recognize her kingdom, I know one thing for certain: she'd embrace all aspects of it, every last detail, and write about them in the only way she could, with love and care, and above all with urgency, pushed by the intent to catalogue everything lest any one missed detail came back to "haunt" her.

I first came across Enid Dame's poetry in the Homecrest
Branch of the Brooklyn Public Library, not far, I learned
years later, from where Enid lived in Brighton Beach. I was
sixteen and searching the shelves for poets long dead or dy-
ing. Instead I came across *Anything You Don't See*. The po-
ems inside talked about Brooklyn. They talked about the
D-train and Brighton Beach, places I've seen, and heard,
and smelled. The poems had a texture of which I knew the
touch. I was completely taken. Enid's poetry accurately de-
scribed the tension one feels growing up in the shadows of
a historic borough, in the shadow of immigrant parents who
perhaps feel even the slightest pangs of being let down: is this
what we struggled for? In the last poem, "Interim Report,"
Enid writes:

> They haven't sold the river yet.
> I can see it from this elevated train,
> slowly unwinding itself
> between islands.
> I tell my dead father.
> He says, "Good, some things they can't get."
> My mother whispers in my other ear,
> "Enjoy it while you can."

Enid did not fight against this history. She did not argue with
the aging socialists who scoffed at the borough and its people
who they may have felt squandered their legacy. In fact Enid
did just the opposite. She took strength in it; she took "root
in [their] imagination." She marveled at the melting pot
that now blended people with the same pasts but different
futures: "The old socialists dislike the new arrivals from Rus-
sia." She took solace in the flux of her place and its people,
in the beach that was her home:

> Here is the ocean. It keeps on breathing,
> sensuous, ragged. A cat on a bed,
> reassuring. It has outlived
> politics and religion.

it has outlived
everything
so far.

Many writers have had their love affair with Brooklyn. And
when Enid died a very beautiful affair went with her. You can
feel its contours in the many letters she wrote Donald Lev
while she lay sick in a Californian clinic. In a stunningly and
quietly sad book published after her death, *Where is the Wom-
an*, Enid's letters to Donald recall and yearn for and measure
a life she lived and loved because of the city in which she
lived and the man in it whom she loved. "I thought of how
I came to New York in 1967," she wrote in August 13, 2003,
"how I always thought I left Baltimore in search of 'the Revo-
lution' or a place where I could 'be a writer.' This was the way
I told the story to myself. But it came to me that I was really
coming to find you: my soul mate, my *bashert*. That was the
real purpose of my journey, poetry and politics was part of it,
but not 'it.'"

I'm sure Donald is eternally grateful for Enid's initial trip
north to Brooklyn. And if the borough could talk, she would
say she is too. And I am grateful for the Homecrest branch
of the Brooklyn Public Library that despite its anemic collec-
tion held one very important volume—Enid's.

But still I wonder what Enid would say to the boys at *The New
York Times* who are just now writing about the "best kept se-
cret" of Brighton Beach—the best spot to eat fresh caviar in
the City? She'd laugh a modest laugh and say, "O boys, we
knew it all along."

5. Enid Dame's Householdry

by Burt Kimmelman

Enid Dame's poems concern themselves with great questions, questions that not only have occupied human thought for thousands of years but also, particularly, have provided a basis for self-discovery. So, it is fair to say that the poems are of great moment. What is so remarkable about them, however, is that they are presented without any sort of pomp or pretense—even when, perhaps especially when, they address confounding scriptural issues (which a great many of them do). There is an intimacy in Dame's poems; they have the ring of natural speech, moreover, and they ground themselves in the objects and events of the everyday. Although her work is of great stature, it is marked by an easy eloquence. And this sense of ease conveys the impression that the poems have not been crafted; yet, if we are paying close attention, we will realize the poems have been assiduously constructed. In keeping with her ability to create a language of breezy contemporaneity, furthermore, Dame establishes in her poems a fundamental tension between the modern and quotidian, on the one hand, and the ancient and monumental, on the other; this tension can be the source of exquisite humor, often, and it is always striking, as well as shrewd and wise. What I find Dame's work does that is most memorable, in any case—whether it is concerned with biblical questions or simply past events, or it is tightly focused on a present moment—is to situate and then dissect eternal, universally human concerns, concerns that are endearingly presented, within a domestic context. I believe that Dame's love of the domestic, and especially what I will call *householdry*, is key to comprehending her entire poetic life and *oeuvre*.

It is important to recognize that Dame's work exists on a human scale though it does not deny the grandeur of the divine. Her poems, therefore—comforting as they are in their air of the familiar—are disarming. Indeed, we are never quite prepared for the depth of a Dame insight, established as it is within the most natural or ordinary of circumstances. Consider, for example, "Untenanted," a poem eulogizing Dame's father, which takes advantage of a typical cityscape, begins in the past, and ends in a palpable, moving present. The poem opens with Dame's persona recalling how she contemplated her father's dead body, soon after his passing, probably in a hospital:

> Standing over
> your uninhabited body,
> Father,
> I kept thinking,
> "The building is still there."
>
> I could picture it: the five-floor Bronx walk-up
> where memory started, for you.

The poem moves through time and details of her father's childhood neighborhood, only to shift to a more recent past when the speaker is a grown woman; then Dame relies on an objective correlative to suggest how the speaker saw her father when they were both adults:

> One wet spring,
> you came to see me.
> I showed you the ocean at the end of my block.
> We stood and watched it, a caged animal,
> shrunken, grey, talking to itself.
> A police car crawled down the boardwalk,
> rain-battered, slow as an insect.
> "The city is dying," you said.

There is a lingering, unavoidable sadness here, as the daughter contemplates the father in his aging. And there is a succinct, gritty resolution of this sadness in the poem's closing lines:

> When you were dying, in another city, I was in the
> next room,

on the phone, arguing with a nurse.
She didn't believe what was happening.

And when I touched you
finally
you felt hard, untenanted,
yet warm,
a brick wall
still holding in the sun.

(*Anything You Don't See* 48-49)

If nothing else, Dame is utterly clear-eyed, but she is also compassionate. And her work never strains for an idea or feeling; rather, to read Dame is to be in a conversation with someone you know, in which, we might suddenly realize, a whole lot is at stake—but the ease, the friendliness, with which the conversation is carried on puts us off our guard, and in the end we may find ourselves crying out for help, to be saved, in that we have been so drawn into the speaker's (and our) existential plight. Such is the nature of fate—a theme underlying virtually all of Dame's work—that it transpires without our being able to prepare for it, to strive to turn it if even obliquely from its direction, as time unfolds.

At the heart of Dame's understanding of fate lies, I think, her vexed relationship with her mother, which manifests in the poems' commentary on or depictions of her, and more subtly in Dame's depicted relationship with her long-time husband (and partner in the poetry tabloid *Home Planet News*) who was, I would say, her soulmate, Donald Lev. Dame's poems can be very funny, most obviously in her many midrashic pieces, in which epic scriptural issues are taken up but with the greatest casualness and in the diction of modernity, just as they can be suddenly devastating in recognizing the darkness in human nature, or at times the light therein; either way they are couched in the quotidian. This writerly strategy allows us to see that what can seem distant or cerebral, usually within the Jewish textual tradition, can become immediate and inescapable. Thus it is that Dame's descriptions of males—mates or fathers—strike me as Lev stand-ins, and, furthermore, the mates (i.e., the Lev substitutes) can serve as stand-ins for a version of Dame's mother, in which the daughter had come to terms with her; very often these men are posed in juxtaposition to some mother figure.

References to mothers and motherhood abound in Dame's poems, often in recreated scriptural settings whose biblical aura is unavoidable, for instance in dramatic monologues like the "Lilith" section of the poem "Looking for a Mother," which begins as follows.

> I never knew my mother.
> We never spoke.
> I knew my father's name
> but never hers.
> The grasses whisper.
> The owl moans faintly.
> The owl is never silent:
> it creaks and hums and scratches.
> Is one of these her voice?

> (*Stone Shekhina* 14)

Likewise, here is "Day 20," a section of "Excerpts from Naamah's Journal":

> The rain beats on the wood
> like my mother's voice pounding pounding:
> Bad girl bad girl bad girl
> Look at this mess! Look at your life!
> You live in a sty you'll never get clean.
> Dirty girl! Dirty! Dirty!

> My mother treated her bread dough
> like a recalcitrant prisoner
> or child   something that had to be punished

40

her hard palm   pounding pounding it down
until it yielded sweetness.
My philosophy was different!
I tried to work with the dough
as if we were partners   colleagues
comrades in a pleasant enterprise.
Of course, we weren't equals:
the bread, eventually, got eaten.
I told myself this was what it wanted.

(*Stone Shekhina* 25)

And yet, when it comes time for Dame's rendezvous, and ultimate showdown with her actual mother, that crucial rapprochement occurs in Dame's own, contemporaneous, unfussy kitchen. Dame confronts her mother there, and seems to forgive her for her unfair treatment, albeit she honors the differences between them. Well, Dame's speaker is smart enough to know not to deny her love for her mother, in this powerful poem of tormented reconciliation:

Yahrzeit

In Jewish tradition, it is customary to light a yahrzeit, or memory candle, on the anniversary of a family member's death.

The *yahrzeit* flame
is beating its wings in a cup
on the edge of my kitchen sink.
Its stealthy gold shadow
breathing along the wall
suddenly terrifies me:
like finding a bird in my bedroom
still alive pulsating nervous,
changing the shape of the day.

No intruder is ever harmless.
And, Mother, I've got you cornered,

41

fierce memory pacing your glass cage,
houseguest with nowhere to go.
I'll lock myself in alongside you.
Today, we'll remind each other
of old connections, old journeys,
from muddy, sincere Indiana
to ragged-edged Brooklyn
with all its stray cats, its ecstatic
vegetable stands.

(*Anything You Don't See* 41)

In Donald Lev's volume *Grief,* made up of poems about Dame's dying of cancer and aftermath, we find this uncomplicated, touching remembrance, in the title poem: "I helped you bathe,/ grateful for the intimacy,/ then we held hands,/ we even joked […]" (*Grief* 9). This poem—this whole collection—is the appropriate counterpart to the letters to Lev and the poems of this period Dame wrote not long before her demise, when she had traveled to California for hyperthermia treatments in a last-ditch effort to be cured, writings Lev collected in the volume he titled *Where Is the Woman.* These inscriptions, these attestations, I believe, document Dame's arrival at a stage of serenity in her relationship with her mother, if not also in her struggle with her fatal disease. Time and again, here, she paints a picture of domestic order, and this picture is consoling, but, in these very late writings, I wonder if Dame has not achieved the ideal human connection with another, in this case her husband, and thereby, through their relationship, some peace.

Her poem "Missing" concludes (starting with the refrain that frames the entirety):

This is a missing-Don letter. Here,
I count the pills myself
imagining you sitting across from me:
your voice   your face   your hands
        opening a bottle,

42

breaking the stillness of the morning.
We talk of poetry or friends or shopping
over bread   cheese   almond butter
fresh blueberries in season.

Because food is a benediction
because sharing food is a sacrament
because shared language is a morning prayer
because I miss the tabernacle
in which our love increases,

it is difficult to eat alone
in this place of healing.

(*Where Is the Woman* np)

Now, compare this passage with Lev's poem "Scene from a Marriage":

So precarious!
Two tipsy piles of books
At the edge of the dresser,
Her reading glasses tucked
In between them.

On my side,
An even tipsier pile
Threatens from the night table.

(*Yesterday's News* 48)

And now consider this stanza from "The Idea of a House" (another of Dame's California poems):

The idea of a bedroom
under a slanting roof
pillows piled high   bright-squared afghan
tower of books on the floor,
long nights read into mornings

waiting for a familiar tread on the stairs;
waiting to be joined.

In this poem, Dame will fully expand Lev's conceit, memori-
alizing the domestic routine she shares with her husband:

The idea of two people
working in separate rooms;
one is fastening down words in wax,
one is cuttling garlic
tomatoes   basil   sorrel if it's spring,
spinach if it's winter,
building the soup
they will eat together, later
meeting at the table.

The poem concludes with the sense of her unvarnished
hope:

The idea of a house
will persist
even when the house is sold
even when the lives lived there,
live elsewhere
and newcomers move in.
They will unpack new words vegetables
          cooking pots.
They will remodel the kitchen.
They will add another chapter
to the house's biography.

They will set up new routines
to sustain them   in the shadows
we leave behind.

(*Where Is the Woman* np)

Overall, I would argue that Dame turns to the scene of do-
mesticity most regularly because this is what she came to prize

most in her life. And in her last poems and letters, published in *Where Is the Woman a*nd elsewhere too, as well as in some of Lev's poems of that period and shortly thereafter, such as we see particularly in his volume *Grief,* we find the domestic—householdry—memorialized. It is within this householdry, furthermore, that Dame establishes with her mate what we can imagine to be her solving of the pain of her relationship with her mother, and we see her triumph in her relationship to Lev.

As I have already suggested (above), Dame is known widely for the remarkable, insightful humor that holds many of her poems together. Madeline Tiger has commented that Dame "expanded the 'story' of our lives by moving us into history, and by bringing history forward—hilariously—into the present" (I.1). Tiger goes on to point out that "[t]here is an ironic vein in Dame's work—embedded in historic paradox. Laughter connects grief and survival" (II.6). All the same, what I find most important in Dame's work is her ultimate reconciliation with the world, which can take the form of a coming to terms with her mother; this repeated scenario is drawn in the sharpest of perspectives. Here, for example, is "Fruit Cellar":

> Bury your memories
> like jars in a fruit cellar.
> Let them mount high on the shelves.
> Let them wait.
> Dark jewels   in their cold nests
> they will keep.
>
> Unbottle them later,
> if you can find that town,
> if you can find that house.
> If anything is left from that time,
> break in. Smash windows,
> lower yourself to the bottom.
> Reach for a memory. Crack one.
> Take what you need.

Now   hold your mother
lingeringly on your tongue.
Her fruit is still alive.
It tastes as it always did:
Heavy   resonant   edgy.
It makes you think of old coats
fur-collared   camphor-scented
worn in another country.

Think of your mother preserving.
Think of your mother destroying.
Her stove: old companion,
turned against herself,
turned into an enemy,
that time she turned on the gas.
Good citizen,
the oven refused to cooperate.
Thirty years later,
she didn't need help to die.

Swallow this memory quickly.
The fruit cellar's silence
isn't empty.
It's a presence,
like a woman's disappointment
stored too long.

It can turn fruit sour,
fracture glass.

(*Anything You Don't See* 36-37)

Still, more subtly, it is Dame's love of the daily living in a
household that tells us of this reconciling, which especial-
ly manifests in the caring descriptions of the husband in a
number of poems, such as in the dramatic monologue "Eve";
Eve's mate's "snores are comforting/ as radiator steam./ My
body is/ the only home/ he hasn't had to leave" (*Stone Shek-
hina* 13).

46

Dame's last poems complete this picture. I will close my re-
flections on Dame's work with the first portion of her very
late poem "Returned" (presumably "returned" from Califor-
nia and her concluding attempt to be rid of her disease):

> This is my kitchen. I am safe here.
> The utensils fit themselves to my hand.
> This blue-speckled pot is an old friend.
> It awaits my pleasures.
> The flame-red casserole with its cracked side,
> its burned-black bottom;
> the quirky veteran propane stove
> are ready for new ventures.
>
> Here I can drink green jasmine tea
> at five AM and feel night drowse itself to daylight,
> the leaves outside are rusty at their edges,
> a sign of coming fall.
> The radio moves from BBC to Mozart.
> My mug is brightly colored:
> a yellow large-eyed cat
> contemplates orange fish,
> while my real cat, fast and black, leaps on the table,
> scraps of cobwebs in his whiskers.
> No one can say he's in the wrong place.
> Everything is right here:
>
> the garlic with its buds snuggled like buttocks,
> the ripening avocado,
> the battered yard-sale colander,
> the square tiles left by a former owner—
> I kept them as they seemed so useful,
> though I seldom use them.
> (*Home Planet News* 13)

Then, finally, there is this passage from another very late,
post-California poem, "Dream at the Start of a Bad Year":

47

There are two elders,
a woman and a man.
She is a poet,
he, a socialist.
They try to change the world
in the little time they live in it.
We share a language
I never learned to speak.

A table spreads between us.
A yard-sale of my treasures:
a rainbow glass   a goblet
with a bubble in its throat
a family of vessels
from the start of memory
back in the Bronx   or Wreschin
(which is now part of Poland).

I must divide these gifts
between my mentors.
(My mother's voice,
and also yours, my love,
advises me
what to bestow on whom.)

A closer look reveals
the legacy is flawed:
the edges chipped   or broken
a crack across the rainbow.

But everything's accepted—
the man impatiently,
the woman, stoic.
The table's almost empty.
A lamp remains: a golden-orange chimney
in which a candle quickens.

I reach to add this offering
to someone's pile: his? hers?

But you say, "No. Not that one.
We have to keep the lamp.
As long as we still live here,
we need the light."

Works Cited

Dame, Enid. *Anything You Don't See.* Albuquerque, NM: West End Press, 1992.

_____. "Dream at the Start of a Bad Year." *Home Planet News 50* [Vol. 12, No. 4] (Spring 2004): 14.

_____. "Returned." *Home Planet News 50* [Vol. 12, No. 4] (Spring 2004): 13.

_____. *Stone Shekhina.* East Hampton, NY: Three Mile Harbor, 2002.

_____. *Where is the Woman?: Letters and Poems from California, July & August 2003.* New York: Shivastan Publishing, 2006.

Lev, Donald. *Grief: Poems by Donald Lev.* Staten Island, NY: Bardpress / Ten Penny Players, 2006.

_____. *Yesterday's News: Poems 1998-2001.* Claryville, NY: Red Hill OUTLOUDBOOKS, 2002.

Tiger, Madeline. "Bless This Garden: A Review of *Stone Shekhina,* Poems by Enid Dame." *The Newark Review* (March 2004), http://web.njit.edu/~newrev/enid/reviews/garden.html.

6. Remembering Enid
by Careufel de Lamière

During the height of what came to be known as the Sum-
mer of Love, 1967, a young man and woman knocked on
my apartment door in Manhattan's east village. They were
political allies in their early twenties, eager, personable and
steadfast in their campaign to end the Vietnam War. I invited
them in, offered them cigarettes and beer (which the man
accepted, accepted and accepted) and for the next five hours
we debated war, peace, art, revolution, love, America and life
itself. It was a marathon meeting of minds. I lost contact with
the man but that day I made what Buddhists term a "heart
connection" with the woman who became Enid Dame, poet,
feminist, editor, spiritual sister, guide and friend.

Looking back over those years I believe Enid did more for
me than I could ever have done for her. She was there when
I kissed my father for the second and last time in my life at
the nursing residence that housed him after his final heart
attack. She was there when I saw my mother alive for the last
time at the final performance of Mayakovsky's *Bed Bug* for
which Enid and I co-wrote lyrics. Less than a week later, we
identified my mother's remains after her death from a fire.
Through it all, Enid was a source of strength, intelligence
and compassion.

To those who had the privilege of knowing her, Enid was
both inspired and inspiring, loving and loved. Her instincts
in politics, poetry and people were always right. Because of
her I secured a job as a caseworker, got a second degree,
backpacked with her in Maine, and helped her place roses
on Emma Goldman's grave in Chicago. We visited Los Ange-
les twice, demonstrated and marched on Sunday afternoon
during the Stonewall Riots, and hitchhiked from Montreal to
Quebec which Enid described in fine poetry she was begin-
ning to get published. She got me my first cat, the magnifi-
cent Alexander the Great Berkman de Lamiere. When I was

hospitalized she visited me more times than I would have visited myself. She enhanced not only my belief in art and humanity but in myself. I will always be grateful to her and I miss her very much. Adieu, ma sœur, mon amie, ma belle. Namaste.

7. On Enid Dame

by Linda Lerner

"Everyone who ever lived brings something into this world that never was and never will be again."

—Martin Buber

Two days after xmas I got another one of those calls, the ones that coincidentally all go back to 2001, have no logical connection with what happened that year, and yet for me, every connection. Another person, gone. The initial shock, it can't be—for this atheist who has trouble believing in death, too—yet always is. This time it was Donald Lev calling to tell me that his wife, Enid Dame, co-editor of *Home Planet News*, his companion of 25 years, died on xmas.

A hundred Enids died as the calls went out that terrible Saturday morning—the person she was with each one of us—and for all—so large, humane, beautiful, repeated like prayers throughout Kalhil Chapel, in Brighten Beach Brooklyn; the day, unusually warm, and sunny for December, comforted and hurt.

These are notes scribbled at an emotional time, for something I planned to write later, when I could think more clearly. Six weeks passed. On re-reading them, I realized that this WAS it. Not "thoughts recollected in tranquility," something logically organized relaying facts, but my reaction following the immediate blow, to allow her spirit to emerge as it did, right then, to me. Yes, "first thought best thought."

The facts of Enid Dame's life, her accomplishments...many... will be noted again and again till everything and nothing of who she is and what I am trying to capture here, and failing so miserably at, is revealed. "I came because of the revolution" she said in one poem I heard her read..."The sound of her being came through in her voice at poetry readings, *Home Planet News* Benefits, classes she taught, in the scream of delight she let out in St. Marks bookstore, the last time we unexpectedly met.

November 2003. I was on my way to see "American Splendor," a film she was deeply moved by, whose significance only became apparent to me, afterwards. There'd be plenty of time for us to get together during the winter break. The film was no longer playing when I got there. The time had past.

We had a closeness that transcended differences in a friendship that began about eleven or twelve years ago. My lover was still alive, and we were both working "with" as he said, not "for" her, in what became for all of us, a job from hell. We survived, went on to attend and participate in her wedding reception to Donald Lev at the Cedar Tavern by reading our poems. Their love enhanced our own, which needed none.

"My god, he was younger than I am!" Enid wrote, expressing shock and much sadness on learning of his death—"another poet's leaving this planet"—about a year before she did. "It seems impossible" she wrote, "that he is not in this world." I can only imagine what uneasy premonitions that news brought.

What else can I say? She was my friend, she is gone now. It seems impossible. There is no replacement. Her husband told me that the illness which led to complications from pneumonia she died from, began about two & a half years ago. Wham…I'm back there again…what my late partner described as, "a year that sucked the life out of many, one way or another," and I referred to in a poem as "a vampire year."

As I'm writing this, I keep hearing Enid cry out through Donald's voice (and I'm paraphrasing..I don't have the poem) is there anyone out there..anyone in all of eternity who can hear me?

It was New Years day, 2004, at the Bowery Poetry Club. Donald, looking lost, somewhat bewildered, spoke about memorials for her, and oh yes, his concern, to ensure he be buried next to his wife.

We who heard her cry out that day, will keep hearing it, and those who'll read the poem, who've never met her will hear it too—the cry of anyone who's ever lived, echoing through eternity.

8. Enid Dame's Voice

by Patricia Markert

Anyone lucky enough to have heard Enid Dame recite her poems in public experienced one of the unique voices in American literature. Enid's genius for transforming a biblical figure into a living breathing contemporary person remains alive, still lives on the page. We can still read her work, but what was lost when she died was her actual voice, the sounds that came out of her when she recited her work, her performing voice. It is a pleasure to follow her sinewy mind as it takes on the personae of characters from the bible, or considers what really happened to Ethel Rosenberg. (Now with new evidence of Ethel Rosenberg's innocence, that particular sestina is increasingly resonant.) How much more we were able to understand though when she read lines like these from "Eve, Much Later," out loud in her inimitable voice:

> I could handle
> losing the Garden,
> losing the deer and wild ducks
> I fed every evening,
> losing the lover
> who raced to me across rivers,
> who taught me to swim
> in and out of water
> (my nimblest companion
> is now an old, achy man
> who won't let me see him naked).

(from *Stone Shekhina*)

When I first knew Enid she was my teacher, leading a writing group in creating midrashic poetry. Easy-going and patient during our sessions, Enid began by reading a passage from the bible in her soft but audible inside-the-restaurant voice (we always met at a Chinese restaurant where Enid discovered the delicious vegetarian dumplings that became a sort of opening ritual before we went to work.) As a teacher she gently suggested, after a careful reading of one of our poems, ways to improve what was begun. And improved it would be.

The resulting poems were published in *To Genesis*, an anthology by Barbara Elovic, Lois Adams, Constance Norgren, and me, with an introductory essay by Enid which opens with these lines:

> The first midrash I ever heard was my mother's. She gave me a perfect, spontaneous introduction to the form in her heartfelt reaction to the story of the Expulsion from the Garden. She took Eve's side and was quite indignant about the matter. "How come everyone blames Eve for Adam's eating the fruit? After all, he was a grown man. She didn't pry his mouth open and force the fruit in!"

Her voice in conversation was solicitous, kind, inquisitive. Her voice was a little high, a little quivery, not exactly lacking in self-confidence, but you would not know to meet her of her accomplishments. If you passed her on the street, you would pick up a hint of a New Yorker who still kept some of her idealism from the sixties, along with her long wavy hair, her comfortable shoes, and her bohemian blouses.

But when she read aloud on stage she commanded the podium. Her voice went down to a more assertive register. There was authority in the low timbre, the clear tone, the immediacy of it all. She dared you not to pay attention. You just had to listen. Not only was the poetry surprising and fresh and alive, the performance had a tone that said, this is important, you don't want to miss a syllable, listen carefully.

If you have ever gone to a poetry reading and found the performance of the reader a huge disappointment, you know that fine poets are not always fine readers. I saw Elizabeth Bishop read once, and felt sorry for her discomfort. Here was a major writer who hated to perform. On the other hand, writers whose voice recordings improved my understanding of their sometimes opaque work are Theodore Roethke and W. H. Auden.

Donald Hall in an essay in *APR* in 2006 wrote, "Poems are for saying aloud, but we usually see them first as black letters set on a page." He had written a year earlier in the same magazine, "Poetry out loud is never quite so beautiful as poetry read in silence. To hear in the mind this sound-beauty, the reader must have read much poetry, learning to love the physical, bodily pleasure of it by an imagination of its presence. [...] A good performer of poetry—seldom an actor— is a lover of poetry who is gifted with a voice that can control potential beauty into actual beauty. Sometimes the poet and the performer can be the same." This was the case with Enid.

Because so many of her poems are written as dramatic monologues, her reading of them takes on an aspect of a one woman show, the way Anna Deveare Smith can take on the roles of many real people she has interviewed. In just such a way does Enid have the authentic voices and troubles and joys of her characters, of Eve, and Sarah, and Noah's daughter, and even the Collier Brothers, in a poem I am not sure is published:

> Our neighbors are the eccentrics,
> inflicting unnatural order—
> with edgers and trimmers
> and gassy weed-whackers—
> on unruly life
>
> ("The Collier Brothers Back Yard")

Often her poems in the midst of being serious have humor.

One of my favorite poems of hers is the "Uses of Laughter," dedicated to her partner and husband and kindred spirit, Donald Lev:

> This is an ancient skill
> our tribe perfected
> in dark European ghettoes:
> like making soup out of stones,
> like nagging the world's conscience,
> like arguing with God.
>
> We were a nation of stand-up comics,
> lawyers, negotiators,
> people who said words mattered.

(from *Anything You Don't See*)

Hearing a voice on tape, like watching an actor on film, brings back the person who has left us, and lets us enjoy her presence again. Donald Lev, in his essay that appeared in the July/August 2008 issue of *Jewish Currents*, quotes from an unpublished poem about the daffodils she planted after September 11. In her words from the poem "Bulbs," "All we'll have is six flowers/ If they actually bloom next spring,/ if we're here to see, to remember."

All we have of Enid now is her work, and our memory of her. I will always miss her physical voice as she stood in front of a crowd to read what she had written—and she was in her glory. Won't someone bring it out of the audiotape in your closet, and make it available to us again?

9. Enid Dame's Legacy
by D. H. Melhem

Before I thought of Enid Dame as a "midrashist" or even un-
derstood the significance of the word, I had a special appre-
ciation of her as a poet and person. The latter first, because
we were classmates in a graduate English class at City Col-
lege in 1971, then became friends via the New York Poets'
Cooperative. Years later, she recalled to me something she
admired that I'd said in class, and I was touched by her gen-
erous assessment as well as by her memory.

Although their writing styles differed, I always associated Enid
with Donald Lev. Their shared lives embraced an indivisible,
nonsectarian humanism and a concern with justice—for
Jews, Christians, Blacks, Muslims, Israelis, Palestinians, Na-
tive Americans, workers, Planet Earth (and other elements
of the universe)—for anyone or anything in need of it. Like
Donald, Enid was intent on maintaining the quality and edi-
torial integrity of *Home Planet News*. It was a "clean, well-light-
ed place" (to recall an Ernest Hemingway story) that, in turn,
illuminated the New York poetry scene, its productivity and
issues, both local and national. Her unmistakable voice, inci-
sive and amusing, beguiles the intellect. When she takes you
gently by the hand, you will dance with her and jump from
stone to stone of composition across an unfamiliar stream.
Your arrival will be nothing like your departure. She has led
you to a new place.

I share Donald's special regard for *Anything You Don't See*
(1992). In "Riding the D-Train," Dame warns, "Anything you
don't see/ will come back to haunt you." Profound com-
ment, conversational tone. A modest and democratic poet,
she wants to be understood. We see her command of craft
growing absolute as she orchestrates each piece, elaborating
on its tone and temper, its associative flow. Theme, prosodic
intention, and a magical tessellating of myth and reality ren-
der her unique vision. She says, "I'm the type of woman who

questions what's easy" ("Ethel Rosenberg: A Sestina"). Alive to our complex of needs, sorrows, and small triumphs, her poetry will endure.

In "Lilith, I Don't Cut My Grass" (*Stone Shekhina*, 2002), the closing poem of her last book, Dame identifies Lilith's uncut hair with her own unmown lawn, and disdains a power mower because she is "terrified of power./ There's too much let loose in the world." Affirming life, she welcomes the weeds, and ends with this invocation: "Lilith, bless this garden/ while both of us still use it." Dame speaks for the rest of us who, though diminished by loss, continue to till the community soil she has enriched and which we also use, for now.

*   *   *

In Tribute to a Pair of Books and to Their Authors:

Where is the Woman: Letters and Poems from California, by Enid Dame (Shivastan, 2006), and *Grief,* by Donald Lev (Ten Penny Players, Inc., 2006)

I've known Enid Dame since graduate school at CCNY in the early 1970s, and Donald Lev since the inception of the New York Poets' Cooperative at approximately the same time. I have always admired them, their poetry, their integrity, and their unstintingly generous contribution to the New York poetry scene through *Home Planet News.* I read their recently published books compulsively, successively as a pair. The singular experience became a kind of open-heart-open-book surgery. I took in the works seamlessly: Enid's desperate attempt at an unconventional cancer cure in California, the story of the couple's great love and loss, and Donald's residue of grief and memory.

Enid Dame's letters reveal the making of several poems, including "Where Is the Woman?" and they present some of her major pieces, most notably, "Wrestling with Angels." A poem of midrash, it incorporates the story of Jacob who "wrestled with an angel" into her own heartbreakingly brave quest:

> I've come to California
> to wrestle with an angel.
> She hasn't shown up yet. I know she's coming.
> Will she drive a Cadillac and vote Republican?
> Will she wear a flowered sundress and drink organic
>   milk?
> Will she be the high school teacher
> I could never please?
> Will she be my mother?

Enid's letters disclose the poet's concern with the right word or phrase or resonance; her respect for Donald's editorial input and poetry. Her high regard for Donald's *Twilight* (CRS Outloudbooks, 1995) affirms the precision of her taste. Enid's poems are exquisitely crafted; "hewn" would be a more appropriate verb for Donald's muscular vision.

Donald Lev's *Grief* responds to Enid's absence in California and her husband's attempt to cope with her death. Among the powerful, reflective poems of this testament, "Shiva," in eleven lines, offers a monumental, Job-infused cry of the heart. It begins:

> They have rent all my garments.
> They make me sit upon the hard wet ground.
> They have sent their children away from me.
> They have crushed my mirrors.
> And they command me to mourn.
> I ought to rejoice in the commandment.
> And I do. I do.

The two books grip the reader with their immediacy, their truth of struggle, grief, and hope, with what they affirm about courage and the devotion to poetry. I would rank them with the finest, most profound renderings of tragic love. Wrench-

61

ing, at times almost unbearably so, yet how gratifying it is that the books exist, in their separate uniqueness. The fit is perfect, the way we hold these poets together in our hearts.

In a poem written for Enid and Don's tenth anniversary in 1994 and read again at the Enid Dame Tribute, celebrated—like the previous event—at the Cedar Tavern, Sunday, March 21, 2004, I remarked, "You learned how to marry your work/ and each other/ distinctly." (*Home Planet News*, Issue 50). Although their poems differ stylistically, the substance of their mutual appreciation and valued critical appraisals remains intact.

Everybody needs to have, to hold, and to read these unique, shattering, inspiring books. They're as indispensable, say (the generous authors would forgive my homely simile), as chicken soup.

10. Enid Dame: Midrashic Prophet
by Alicia Ostriker

Once upon a time there were women prophets. Really. Well, there were at least three of them. We have their names in the Bible: Miriam is called a prophetess in Exodus 15, where we see her leading the women of Israel in song and dance on the Red Sea shore after the escape from Egypt. Deborah, a prophetess and judge (and commander-in-chief) in Judges 4-5, is responsible for the defeat of the Philistine general Sisera, and sings a triumphal song about this. Huldah shows up briefly in Kings 2 as a prophetess consulted when "the book of the law" is found in the ruins of the destroyed temple. She predicts that divine judgment will fall on Judah for forsaking god, but that the faithful king Josiah would die in peace before that happened.

It isn't a great record, if you think about the millions of words attributed to Jeremiah, Isaiah, Ezekiel, and company. All those eloquent mouthpieces of a God who says we should seek justice, feed the hungry and clothe the naked, care for widows and orphans, and so on, and who is also (by the way) the Supreme Egotist for whom nothing, but nothing, is more important than getting worshiped. For those who don't worship Him, genocide is a good solution.

Now fast forward…and maybe we need some new solutions? Maybe we need some new prophets?

I nominate Enid Dame. It seems to me she is very well qualified for the job. One: she is strong on social justice issues and speaking truth to power, but not a big fan of holy war. Two: she is a very good Jew in my sense of the word. She honors her father and mother and all her ancestors, and has an abiding respect for nature. Three: she is tender-hearted. Four: she has a great sense of humor.

You think that's not enough? Well, how about this: she is the first woman poet to undertake a re-imagination of Jewish

63

mythology—which means she is the first to re-imagine our relationship to God. And she first does this in a sequence of nine bawdy, bold, and brilliant poems published in 1989 under the title *Lilith and her Demons*. Because they are so entertaining, you might not realize how revolutionary these poems are. So let me explain.

But first a word about feminist midrash. I and others have spent a fair amount of time in the last twenty years wrestling midrashically with the book we sometimes fondly call the Old Testicle. Midrash lets us take tales that feature a male God and male patriarchs, warriors, judges, priests, kings, and prophets, and spin the tales differently from the way they have been spun by two thousand years of male rabbis, theologians and scholars.

In my own reading of scripture, I assume that the being we call God the Father swallowed God the Mother in prehistory, like the wolf in the folk tale swallowing grandmother. But just as grandmother doesn't die, so She—the Great Goddess, with her many names, including Sophia and Shekhinah—does not die, cannot die. She is right there inside God's belly. Sometimes we can see her kicking—which is to say we can see the textual traces of her repressed memory. For God is not dead, God is not dying, He's just pregnant…and it is our task to help him give birth to the holy female in him. Where did I start to get these weird ideas? Ask Enid. Her Lilith poems were the jump-start for me.

According to several scholars the figure of Lilith—Adam's first wife, who refused to lie beneath him during sex, and flew off to make her home by the Red Sea—may be a vestige of a Mother-goddess religion. Throughout the middle ages Lilith was a feared and hated succubus; she was believed to seduce Jewish men and make demons out of their sperm to torment mankind. Orthodox Jewish households still protect their homes with amulets against the baby-killing powers of Lilith. In other words: Lilith is a male fantasy figure representing the attractiveness and horribleness of autonomous female sexuality. And you think this fantasy is not still with us? Oy.

In the first poem of Dame's sequence, simply entitled "Lilith," this early rebel "kicked myself out of paradise" after some quarrels with Adam:

> he carried a god
> around in his pocket
> consulted it like
> a watch or an almanac
>
> it always proved
> I was wrong
>
> two against one
> isn't fair! I cried
> and stormed out of Eden
> into history...
>
> now
> I work in New Jersey
> take art lessons
> live with a cabdriver
>
> he says: baby
> what I like about you
> is your sense of humor

We notice right away that Lilith has a clear sense of justice and fairness, spells god with a lower-case g as if there were more than one of them, is inclined to make fun of legalism, prefers independence and creativity to subordination and posh living quarters, and is (of course) immortal. What we might call an archetype. A down-to-earth archetype with a sense of humor, which should remind us that a sense of humor is one of the things missing from most concepts of God, but is also one of things most useful as a survival strategy, especially for Jews. But Lilith isn't just a smartypants, and she isn't a male-basher either. The poem ends by telling us

> Sometimes
> I cry in the bathroom
> Remembering Eden
> And the man and the god
> I couldn't live with

—which endows this immortal being with a vulnerability and tenderness we wish we could attribute to our male divinities.

In the sequence's second poem, Dame leaps forward to "Lilith at the Abortion Clinic," to let us know that "this has been happening for centuries." Then comes one of my all-time favorites, "Lilith and Eve." Lilith, who confesses she's been "married twice/ divorced a thousand times" over the centuries, meets Eve "at a tenants' rights rally/ at Dag Hammarskold Plaza" and they bond, though Eve "seemed to feel/ one of us/ should act guilty." Eve has joined a women's consciousness-raising group and explains Adam "was unsupportive. 'You know how he is.'" Well, we do know. He's the old Adam. Even funnier and sadder is the last time Lilith has seen him—in a Brooklyn dairy restaurant; "that time around he was/ an orthodox Jew:"

> He washed his hands   said a prayer
> Before talking to me
> Wouldn't touch me
> Not even shake hands
> Because we weren't married

And when Lilith asks how Eve is doing, he evades and recommends the baked whitefish. What I love here is that behind the comedy Dame is critiquing orthodoxy as a closed system that diminishes human kindness. I think she's right. Likewise, in "Lilith Talks About Men," Dame nails the fear and hatred of women and sex that underpins patriarchy:

> they all have
> desires
> they can't find words for
>
> the way I see it
> I give them
> a gift   of sweat and hair
> the only thing I know
> worth giving
>
> they see it
> differently   when
> it's over
> they hate me
> . . . .
> the names they call me
> haven't changed
> in 4,000 years

A couple of poems later, "Lilith's Talent" addresses the specific canard that she mothers demons. As she tells it, yes, she breathes "ripples of life/ into unwanted sperm," mothering "energy,/ the unpredictable spark/ into a world/ that needs it:"

> Oh men of religion
> with your amulets, your chants,
> your direct-mail campaigns:
> stop telling lies to yourselves!
> you move through a world
> filled with angels
> you helped me create.
>
> But you insist
> on calling them
> demons.

It seems to me this comes very close to what that other prophetic rebel, William Blake, is doing in *The Marriage of Heaven and Hell*—radically reversing what pious people see as "good" and "evil," claiming that erotic energy is what Blake called "Eternal Delight." Blake spent a lifetime combating the Christian view of sex as sin. Jewish tradition doesn't exactly label sex sinful, but Christian anxieties and repressions have certainly leaked into Judaism—see Daniel Boyarin's wonderful book *Carnal Israel* on this topic. Dame's view of sex is closer to what we find in the biblical Song of Solomon, where the lovers are plainly unmarried, the woman is equal to the man, and sex is something like what Rabbi Akiva called a Holy of Holies.

Yet unlike Blake, and unlike most other feminist women poets (including me) writing against the patriarchal order, Dame doesn't seem to get hot under the collar. Her best weapon is gentle mockery. Even in "Lilith's Sestina," a poem that deals with male power as a destructive force that (with the help of male writers who revile women) may destroy the planet, she registers the danger, but hesitates to be absolutist about anything. "Men," she says, "crash through the world like proprietors, never doubting their right/ to trample, to resurrect. But for me, wrong and right/ blur like the sky's edge on ocean."

Wouldn't we like to see our governments do a little more of this blurring and a little less announcing that everybody else is either with them or against them? Wouldn't we like to have religions a little less preoccupied with righteousness, and more into love? Wouldn't we like to live in a world that wasn't so woman-hating? Well, that is what prophets are for. They challenge the state, the church (or synagogue), and the society. They imagine beyond where we are to how we might live under our vines and fig trees with nobody making us afraid. But speaking of ocean, the final poem in *Lilith & her Demons* backtracks to the time of Noah and puts Lilith on the ark, sweetening the dreams of both men and women, say-

ing she "wouldn't have missed/ this trip for the world." So
Dame exits this book not with protest, not with polemic, but
with her characteristic fondness for life.

That fondness animates all of Dame's work. Her death was
horribly untimely. But her spirit is timeless. Anyone who
met Enid, or read her or studied with her, or was her col-
league or taught her poetry, will hold her dear. We know
what a shining and funny person she was, how she could be
so right without ever being righteous, how the landscape of
her work was a cross between Brooklyn and Paradise. Her
midrashic writing is a tree of life sprouting through disas-
ters. Her writing as a whole is sharply political without being
simple-minded, passionate and humane without sacrificing
playfulness. May her work continue to ripple out her lefty
spirit of truth and compassion and comedy and justice and
life. May it live and be healthy.

11. Enid Dame and the Hudson River Valley
by Judith P. Saunders

A long-time Brooklyn resident who moved from the city in mid-life to make her home in High Falls, New York, Enid Dame has left a significant poetic record of her engagement with the Hudson Valley. Her perspective on the region is neither simple nor typical, for she brings to bear upon her topic a sensibility that is urban, Jewish, and feminist. She conjures up flora, fauna, and landscape with an accurate eye, conveying the flavor of rural village life, but she remains poised between outsider and insider points of view. Her interest in Jewish history and legend permeates her experience of the place, moreover. Even as she evokes immediate details of her physical surroundings, details replete with homely credibility, she infuses these with the larger significance of myth. Readers will find her view of the Hudson Valley at once unpredictable and authentic; her poems describe a place reconstructed by imagination yet wonderfully recognizable.

On a simple narrative level, Dame's poems recount a familiar saga: New Yorkers acquire a country place north of the city to which they escape on weekends for relaxation and refreshment, gradually spending more and more time there until the country retreat becomes the primary place of residence. In a poem called "Innocence," Dame recalls how she and her husband "would turn our backs on the city/ those jaunty Fridays" (lines 4-5). Driving into the night, they stop for groceries "in the village cradled by the Catskills," finally pulling into a "sleeping street" and preparing a "midnight dinner" that is a "feast" (8, 23, 24, 29). The adjective "jaunty" clearly underlines the happy, adventurous spirit of the weekend trips. Even the long, dark drive is filled with suspense as they enter the majesty of the landscape: "the mountains were waiting for us" (6). They can "smell in the dark" their aromatic "yard full of weeds and flowers" (22, 21). On "lush evenings" tinged with natural magic, they revel in stars that seem "nearer, fiercer than Brooklyn's" (12, 13).

Dame describes the house in High Falls as "sagging," filled with a "cargo of spiders [and] mice"; even the water flowing from the kitchen tap contains "various wormy and spidery additions" ("Innocence" 17, 18; "Miriam's Water" 9). Inside and out, this country dwelling-place offers urban newcomers an environment bristling with raw, natural vitality; it is "a house/ with a broken screened-in-porch,/ a wild grapevine spreading inside" ("The Idea of a House," 1-3). The poet rejoices in her "backyard/ where it's always cool and ferny,/ where jewelweeds grow taller than trees" ("Lilith, I Don't Cut My Grass" 3-5). She allows weeds to flourish side-by-side with tomatoes, marigolds, and roses, discovering in the wild and tangled growth a primal source of life-affirming health. She imagines that the unfettered growth she has fostered is under the special protection of Lilith, a Hebrew figure of mythic stature: "I don't cut my grass/ as you never cut your hair;/ I picture you in my backyard….Lilith, bless this garden" (1-3, 54). Dame invokes this figure from Hebrew mythical tradition to assert feminist concerns in tandem with ecological ones. She compares the rampant fertility of her High Falls garden, "gone wild," to untamed female force ("The Idea of a House," 5): social expectations work to "burn all the wilderness" out of girls' bodies and spirits, but here the deliberately "uncut grass" and "flaunting…purples" reflect a more unconstrained version of the womanly self ("Lilith, I Don't Cut My Grass" 22; "The Idea of a House," 8).

Elsewhere Dame invokes the Old Testament figure of Miriam to describe the special "sweetness" of the water she drinks in High Falls ("Miriam's Water" 10). Despite the occasional insect-laden residue, this water from "a well shared with two neighbors" tastes deliciously refreshing in comparison with the "bland" liquid drawn from city reservoirs ("My Relationship with Water" 8). "The sweetness was a marvel, a gift," she explains; "coffee here had more echoes than Brooklyn's" (15, 16). Drinking a cool glassful on a hot day is "a fuller experience," like hearing "a live symphony" in place of "a song on the radio" (18, 19). Enjoying water direct from its earthy sources, she thinks of the Israelites to whom, through Miriam, God reveals water in the desert: "your [Miriam's] well...sweetened their bumpy journey" ("Miriam's Water" 21). She likens her own family's "small wanderings" to that Old Testament Exodus, identifying "this house/ at the bottom of its mountain" as the end-point of the journey (26, 27-28). The "half rhyme" or "sound imagery" linking this village on the west side of the Hudson River with her place of origin—Beaver Falls, Pennsylvania—makes the move to High Falls seem right ("Names," 5). She feels at home here, more fully "real" than ever before: "buoyed by your water, Miriam,/ I'm taking on substance" ("Miriam's Water" 39, 36-37). Thus she pays tribute to the elemental resources persisting in the Mid-Hudson valley: it is a place in which refugees from the metropolis can re-establish a relationship with nature. Her poems define the region in terms of nature's energy and beauty, life-giving and indeed, miraculous: *a marvel, a gift.*

Even as she celebrates peace, bounty, and renewal in her rural home, however, Dame points to encroaching threats. Though far from the regimented grid of Manhattan's streets, "neighbors are complaining" about her unkempt yard ("Lilith, I Don't Cut My Grass" 36). Instead of admiring this display of burgeoning life, "they're collecting money/ to buy me a power mower" (37-38). A peaceful place is invaded by the specter of condominiums ("sucking up the sun") and by "chemicals"—because even here there's "no room for weeds" (50, 52, 53). Sadly, too, the water whose "personality" and "sweetness" so amazes her proves subject to pollution. She had been willing to cope with cracked pipes and eccentric plumbing, with the after-effects of storm when "water acrobats out of the ceiling" or "swims backward in the hall,/ breaking rules like a gang of teenage vandals" ("My Relationship with Water" 26-27). Over time, however, "as the house and we aged together," the water takes on a slightly different taste (31). Suddenly the village water is pronounced unsafe: "a factory up the road, now dead and emptied,/ bled years of debris into the common source" (35-36). As a result, the well water is "rejected and sick," like "a relative driven mad by the doings of others" (41, 42). High Falls is no longer an uncomplicated country village, whose residents live life close to its sources; now they see "all the dangerous springs cemented over" (49). "We'll pay water taxes and become a tiny city" (50). The "quirky" water of the region, to be replaced by a "bland and harmless," relentlessly standardized liquid, will lose its marvelous quality (51, 50).

Thus Dame's appreciation of the Hudson Valley is tinged with the recognition that the refuge it provides is vulnerable. All its spaciousness and bounty are provisional. At the same time that she grapples with the environmental degradation threatening her country home, moreover, she regards the city she "abandoned" with an affection deepened by the events of September 11, 2001 ("Innocence," 41). The great metropolis she was so ready to escape has proved vulnerable, itself, beyond all imagining. "Struck down," it is like "a fragile relative" now "claiming all our energies" and "our love" (42, 44, 45). There is no "safe" and "enchanted" place of retreat, she tells herself, asking: "why did I think/ ...that the cloud of burning buildings, burning lives/ would not follow us upstate and everywhere?" (36, 35-36). Looking at an old photograph of Brooklyn Bridge with "the slender Towers/ off-center in a corner," she notes that they are buildings she "never liked/ architecturally" but whose "death" she nonetheless mourns ("Balance" 54-55, 44-45, 43). "Poking up offhandedly" and "heedlessly/ into the naked air,/ so obviously in need of protection," they leave her contemplating, in their absence, a "depleted skyline" (56-58, 61).

Thus her odyssey into a rural paradise "cradled by Catskills" comes full circle, with the acknowledgement that neither city nor country is exempt from hazard ("Innocence," 8). Historically cherished as a place of healthful recreation and retreat, the Hudson Valley is exposed, as she discovers, to problems confronting urbanites dwelling one hundred miles to the south. The after-effects of industrial activity, of international violence, and of housing booms, for example, will leech into the soil, foul the river, and overburden the Mid-Hudson economy, changing the face of its landscape. Her own illness hammers home Dame's realization with extra force: there is no place, no matter how seemingly idyllic, secure from the ever-present threat of mortality. She suggests a possible response to this recognition of dangers and limits in a poem written before she left Brooklyn, "Interim Report," in which she stakes stock of her life in early middle age. She begins and ends the poem with the Hudson River, an often overlooked feature of the cityscape: "Boys fish in the hot river/ along the city's flank," is her opening observation. Reflecting in the body of the poem on political and economic forces she cannot challenge decisively, she wryly notes that "they haven't sold the river yet," ending with an admonition (32):

> I can see it from this elevated train,
> slowly unwinding itself
> between islands.
> I tell my dead father.
> He says, 'Good, some things they can't get.'
> My mother whispers in my other ear,
> 'Enjoy it while you can.' (33-39)

Paradise is always receding or collapsing; every newfound utopia is subject to disintegration or invasion. To counter inevitable decay, of person or of place, there is only one response, Dame suggests: to accept the gifts of the moment without reservation. She concludes the poem "Miriam's Water" with a wonderful image of herself as a transparent container, or receptor, for the natural wonders surrounding her: "I'm real as this windowsill bottle/ holding a piece of the sky/ lightly, between its walls" (39-41). In these lines written to commemorate her special feeling for the Hudson Valley, she finds a perfect balance between the opposite poles of her awareness, allowing the boundaries between self and nature to become almost mystically invisible.

Works Cited

Dame, Enid. *Anything You Don't See.* Albuquerque, NM: West End Press, 1992.

———. "Balance." And Then 12 (2004): 66.

———. "The Idea of a House." Where Is the Woman? 7-8.

———. "Innocence." Unpublished manuscript (owned by Donald Lev).

———. "Interim Report." *Anything You Don't See.* 50-51.

———. "Lilith, I Don't Cut My Grass." *Stone Shekhina.* 66-67.

———. "Miriam's Water." *Stone Shekhina.* 5-6.

———. "My Relationship with Water." *Bridges* 12.1 (2007): 53.

———. "Names." *Phoebe* 8.1-2 (Spring / Fall 1996): 178.

———. *Where Is the Woman? Letters and Poems from California.* Woodstock, NY: Shivastan, Publishing, 2006.

———. *Stone Shekhina.* East Hampton, NY: Three Mile Harbor, 2002.

12. Two Brief Testimonies

I've been reading and rereading "Lilith at the Cloisters," a poem I've loved for awhile. There's so much of Enid in there, and I hear her voice very clearly: innocent and wicked and curious, all at once. Her innocence (which seems so unusual) sprang out of her rare delight in things, and they didn't have to be weird or bent out of shape to catch her eye—I know a cat pouncing could just do it.

Susan Sindall

My admiration for Enid is simple, but she was wonderfully complex, the line of her life intersecting with many other lives, weaving a silk of the spirit that was beautiful and colorful and glowing, gathering love & poetry, and through her own poetry and publishing she was an important agent of social change, and her effects will continue beyond us.

Harry Smith

13. Enid: In Remembrance

by Maxine Susman

In the late '80s, Enid and I worked together in the Rutgers Writing Program in New Brunswick, as teachers and campus-wide administrators. It was a busy job, and because she didn't call attention to her creative life, I didn't know she was a poet until she gave a reading at Douglass College in a room packed with fans. Over the years I saw the same transformation many times from a down-to-earth, completely unpretentious person into a reader whose quirky public voice and welcoming smile summoned the many alter egos she created to speak for all of us. She clearly enjoyed this kind of ventriloquism, finding words to reveal lives. I came to know that Enid herself lived many identities aside from her academic day job—poet, feminist, Jew, intellectual, leftist, peace activist, human rights advocate, and (let's not forget) humorist.

When my sister and a close friend developed breast cancer at the same time in 1995, I started writing poetry again. I showed a few poems to Enid. She read with kindness and enthusiasm, because it was her nature to do so, never mentioning she herself had been ill. As she did for many others – peers, friends, students—she helped rekindle the poetry spark in me; my first published poem appeared in *Home Planet News.*

A few years later, at the New Jersey College English Association, someone in the audience of our poetry panel asked Enid whether she thought an MFA or English graduate credential was important for someone wanting to be a poet. Enid's response was refreshingly direct: she had loved poetry since childhood, it was a natural human activity, and there were different ways to come to it. No one at any level should feel inadequate, excluded or intimidated; and a good place to start was on one's own, simply reading, listening, and writing poems. This advice, typical of her straightforward inclusiveness, seems central to her life and her writing.

Over the years I went to other Enid readings, at Rutgers, the *Home Planet News* benefits at the Cedar Tavern in the Village, NJCEA. My sister, my daughter, and many women friends knew and loved her work. Once, after a reading at Middlesex County College, a group of us brought her down to Highland Park for a second reading at the old Cleo's Café, where we got to hear Midrashic favorites like "Eve," "Eve Much Later," "Lilith, I Don't Cut My Grass," "Noah's Daughter," and "Hagar: After the Commune Collapsed," twice in one day.

In April 2003, not long after the publication of *Stone Shekhina*, I invited Enid to give the annual poetry reading for National Poetry Month at Caldwell College, the small suburban New Jersey Catholic College where I teach. With Donald sitting in the front row, she read some of the same poems she'd read to her mostly Jewish, middle-aged women friends at the café. I didn't know how the audience of young Catholics would respond to Midrash, if the Jewish humor and sensibility would escape them, if they might be baffled by the concept of retelling Scripture or even offended at hearing her female characters challenge God and divine authority. But they loved her—bemused at first, then charmed, provoked, and persuaded to see religious stories in a novel way that gave voice to the silenced and overlooked.

It is harder than I thought to write a public tribute to the work of a friend and mentor. What can be said about Enid's poems seems redundant in light of the poems themselves, so I will simply to point out some qualities of her work. First, she confounds then and now, ancient and contemporary, to come upon surprising emotional discoveries, as in these lines from "Eve," who now lives with Adam on the Upper West Side:

> His snores are comforting
> as radiator steam.
> My body is
> the only home
> he hasn't had to leave....

> He never will
> forgive me.

She turns comfortable expectations on their heads: according to Noah's Daughter, life aboard the Ark was better than life on land, since her mother transformed it into a nurturing female space of animal talk and comfort food:

> She held me. Her heart beat along with the ocean's.
> At these times,
> the dark Ark felt safe.
> At these times
> I wanted the forty days to go on forever.

An example from "Foreward: Jerusalem Syndrome" shows the Jewish feminist's hope for the coming of Shekhina, the female embodiment of God, in the humorous, human-scale here-and-now:

> I should have known:
> you're still in exile,
> perhaps in upstate New York
> working quietly in a back room
> of a Health Food Co-operative.

Enid saw poetry not as a personal escape from public life but as political statement, a commentary on the world as each person experiences it. Her Midrashic and other poems investigate actions and feelings in order to locate an ethical, activist response both in intimate relationships and in a larger social context. This is the last stanza of "The War Moves Closer," published in *Home Planet News* on the eve of the invasion of Iraq:

> Anxiety sags like snow on the roof.
> I call the number; the line is jammed.
> The President says, "We don't need the world."
> The war moves closer. We try to stop it.

Enid's poems bring everyone together like the human and animal family on the Ark, or as she writes in "Miriam's Seders": "I am like everyone else in the room./ We are all, all the children in the story."

I taught Enid's Eve poems at Duksung Women's University in Seoul recently, during the 2007-2008 Winter Session. It was my first trip to Korea, to Asia for that matter, and I was there on an exchange through Caldwell College to teach a course on Fairy Tales and Children's Literature. My students were eight young women with majors from pharmacy to Spanish, but all enrolled first and foremost to improve their English, which the Koreans consider the ticket to upward mobility. First we read classic Western fairy tales like Cinderella, Red Riding Hood, Rapunzel, works my students all knew at least in their Walt Disney incarnations. Then, American folk heroes mostly unfamiliar to them, Pocahantas, John Henry, Johnny Appleseed, which we compared to traditional Korean tales for the light shed on cultural values and gender expectations. Along the way students wrote and read their own retellings, Midrashic-style, blending western and Korean motifs, creative writing being quite a different challenge from the theme-style papers they were usually assigned.

We spent the last week on children's Bible stories. The class was a mix of Buddhists, Christians, and non-believers, none of whom had met a Jew before, so I fielded questions about customs, foods, holidays, and "why Jews are so rich and powerful." The students already knew the conventional representation in the *Book of Genesis* of the Adam and Eve story: woman's weakness, man's disobedience to God, exile from Paradise. Then we read Enid's poems, listening to Eve tell her own story, with her feminist critique of Adam, God, and her intellectual "playmate," the serpent. To honor these stories in the retelling, so that they make sense of our own lives, was what I had learned from Enid and why I wanted to teach her poems in Korea. I wanted students to hear women in the Bible speak in their own voices, just as I was eager to hear my students speak in theirs, interpreting personally what they learned about Western stories and story-telling.

It has only been since the 1980s—one generation—that Korean women in numbers have gained access to higher education, professional training, jobs outside the home, and non-traditional gender roles. The educational system rewards demonstration of mastery of acquired knowledge, and students have less opportunity for individual self-expression in an academic setting. Yet these young women were very curious about other cultures, about my life in the USA, about the many alternative ways to be in the world; they are eager to explore, investigate, consider different perspectives from the vantage point of their own. Very much like Enid. Here was Enid's middle-aged, Jewish New York Eve, talking to young Koreans in a women's college classroom in a working-class neighborhood of Seoul—would it be a dialogue?

In the spirit of Enid's work, rather than appropriating the students' voices I will give them space to speak for themselves. Here is Jin as Eve: "I wonder how sweet the apple's taste./ If I could take just one bite of an apple,/I [would] feel just like a heaven." And Hye-In speaking as the serpent in a poem she called "Intellectually Alive": "Everything has two sides/good or not/They should know that truth..../the ability to make questions...." And here is Jung Ran in a poem about Eve torn between her two males, Adam and the snake:

> I ate the fruit,
> Adam follows me...
> I have done it of my own free will...
> I am set free
> Turning the fruit into wings
> I fly on the wings to a new world....

These writers infuse the story with their own situations as young women who want to take control of their lives, learn through new experiences, sample otherness. There is also a move toward empowerment through language, a breaking through the difficulty of expressing ideas and feelings in the foreign tongue of English. They enact the Midrashic plan of finding hidden surprises in language and story, of reframing old stories to discover fresh meaning.

When Donald called on Christmas and Chanukah 2003 to tell me Enid had just died, I was shocked and grief-stricken. Such a loss! A gentle, strong, committed soul, a good friend. No new Enid poems. But certainly the poems we have celebrate, remonstrate, affirm, question, amuse and prod, give us the generously human wherever and whenever it reveals itself. A few summers ago at a poetry workshop at the Fine Arts Work Center in Provincetown, each participant took a turn reading some favorite poem. I read "Lilith, I Don't Cut My Grass." "Enid Dame!" cried out a young woman from Washington, D.C. "I love her work!" So I'll close with a quote from that, one of Enid's funniest and best-known poems:

> Lilith, neighbors are complaining.
> They're collecting money
> to buy me a power mower.
> How can I tell them
> I'm terrified of power?
> There's too much let loose in the world.
> It's one gift I don't need....
>
> Lilith, bless this garden
> while both of us
> still use it.

14. A Brief Testimony
by Karen Swenson

I am one of the unlucky ones who didn't know Enid Dame well. I knew her, how shall I say, publicly, through readings and parties and such. Physically she was both an imposing woman and one who gave off waves of humility. When I heard her read I never felt that she was setting her self up before us as the latest poetic tidbit but just as a woman who was coming to life with certain insights, a woman who saw things from a certain angle of perspective.

That angle was always refreshing. My favorite is the rogue female take of the Lilith poems. She makes Lilith into a wondrous wanderer who while sympathetic to Eve is also acutely aware of Adam's and all other sanctimonious male short comings. I've been teaching Lilith for years now. She invariably brightens up a class room like a red tulip in February.

When Enid Dame died I went to her memorial at the Cedar Tavern and watched the crowds of admirers, students, friends, and other poetry practitioners flood in. They were a statement about who she was.

15. Bless This Garden
A Review of *Stone Shekhina*, Poems by Enid Dame
by Madeline Tiger

> Note, from the prelude to the text of this collection: "…the Shekhina…stood for an independent, feminine divine entity prompted by her compassionate nature to argue with God in defense of man."
>
> —Raphael Patai, quoted by Enid Dame

1.

Enid Dame's argument with God was the gentlest we ever knew. *Stone Shekhina,* most recent of Dame's seven collections, is full of memorable characters, most of them constructed out of Biblical texts, apocryphal study, and the poet's amazing imagination. Her strong poems, her unsentimental view of Biblical horrors, and her powerful wit, face us with the mysteries of the Infinite and the terrible realities of our world. Yet her work is an absolute celebration—of history, of quotidian life, and of language, the Word, its power—to remake the world, to enlarge wonder, to make deep sense, and to honor love. Enid expanded the "story" of our lives by moving us into history, and by bringing history forward, hilariously, into the present. As the *Old Testament* Miriam says, (according to Enid's telling):

> We are all, all the children in the story.
> A nation of children sits down at the tables
> for the time it takes to revisit the story,
> which changes as we move through our lives,
> changes us as we move through it together…
> (from "Miriam's Seders")

Dame's poems embody paradox—pre-history and the present simultaneous, traditional learning and revolutionary at-

84

titudes in synchrony; cynicism and hopefulness, furious criticism and great love, all cohering. Enid was a life-long rebel, and yet her voice—in person as on the page—was always full of appreciative humor, tinged with surprise. She produced work reflective of exactly who she was: outraged, yet open-hearted, proud but uniquely generous, critical yet loving. Never judgmental, the poet found herself merged into the world she recreated.

The very concepts Enid started her poems with are hilarious: that Noah had a spunky daughter who could speak to us, that Lilith has an on-going life through centuries and speaks to us; that Jephthah's Daughter could sing both praise and lament before her sacrifice; that Miriam can be critical of her tribesmen, or family... Then come the blazing details, suddenly making the stories immediate, as they mix exotic silliness with old-fashioned nostalgia: Enid has Noah's daughter answer some ridiculous rabbinical questions about the Ark, so she tells about her mother: "I see her in the tiny, sweaty kitchen/ chopping up pieces of seaweed/ making soup out of salt water and discarded shells/ (Meat was forbidden, of course.)/ A spider monkey hung by its tail over her improvised stove..." She goes on in admiration, "My mother spoke animal language./ Not all the dialects—just a few./ Leopard and llama were her favorite./ She could also hoot like an owl..."

"How was the ark lighted?" the final section of the poem begins. "It wasn't. It was a dark, musky cave./ At night I'd crawl in on my mother's side of the bunk./ She'd sing songs to me in her throat. I made her tell me stories..." And finally, "Beside us, Father snored./ She held me. Her heart beat along with the ocean's. At these times, the dark Ark felt safe./ At these times/ I wanted the forty days to go on forever."

85

2.

The characters are "real" for us: we will keep Noah's daughter among us, wistfully dreaming of her cozy days beside her mother on the Ark; and we will know "Miriam's Water," as if she had truly offered it to the poet in High Falls, New York. We will know Esther's triumph and Dina's ironic secret, bitter yet marvelous. With her typical witty slant, Enid taught us how Eve must have wanted to protect Adam from an accusing God. Through "Miriam's Seders" we understand the feminist re-invention of ancient religion: "On the desert/ we cemented our relationship/ with the God we never saw—/ a bit like learning to lean against the air./ If you do it correctly, you'll never fall/ spinning, dizzy, into inner space./ No, you'll learn how to pick up your bags/ and keep moving."

Stone Shekhina is centered on the Noah story—from the point of view of Noah's children, the familiar myth becomes eerily relevant to modern conditions, modern mentalities. It includes a long portrayal of Noah's wife: "Excerpts from Naamah's Journal" uses an authentically detailed narrative style to move from bread-making to rape, survival, despair, and prayer—not a prayer to "the God he won't let me speak to" but to the ocean itself. In "Japeth" the youngest son speaks, centuries later: "I was the boy on the boat/ but then the world turned over./ Today I'm the man in the house./ It's a large box, but I keep it powered.../ My sons are doing well: one's in banking/ one's in computers one's in media./ They hunt together on weekends." And he protests about revealing the past: "My daughter keeps trying to interview me/ for her oral history project./...Why should I spill my guts about Pop's drinking problem Mom's suicide/ her obsession with animals his compulsion to save the world?/ Sure, we were a dysfunctional family...Does the world really need/ another sad story?...Don't stir up old waters./ You'll give yourself nightmares." The poem continues on into more eerie territory of the mind.

Noah's daughter, completely imagined by the poet, as real as any 20th Century girl, becomes a central spokesperson in this series, but many impressive women speak as part of the human circle. We suffer with Jephtha's (unnamed) daughter, stunned by her father's inscrutable cruelty, her love of the detailed world—foods, music, and dance, knowing "This is/ the last night on the mountain./ He let me breathe the air/ for two months before he'll cut it off/ forever. Something's wrong here./ But I can't name it." We can!

We are given glimpses of pre-history, swiftly updated with contemporary references. In "Eve, Much Later," the first woman talks to us: "I could handle/ losing the Garden" and "losing the lover/ who raced to me across rivers…" She accepts losing her own body "(supple and full of teeth) that had shaped me for years,/ even losing the children/ I pushed out of it…without a rulebook." But her great lament is for the snake, "…the friend of my mind the playmate/ whose wit flashed and kindled my own." Wit was her excitement and her essence. "Words were the way we touched/ steel hitting flint…"

Perhaps 20th Century social changes have clarified women's rightful equality, taking her identity with Intelligence for granted; but to go back into the "Beginning," to the woman in The Garden (whom some would still call culpable), to let her declare herself—"We were the world's doctors/ its scientists its comedians"—this is the revolutionary genius of Enid Dame. And then, to have this original Woman declare that where she lives "now" (eons later), she has learned to find and use knowledge, but has no "friend to help me/ stand back and observe it,/ play with it label it/ And make jokes at its expense…" To have such a companion is the wish (expectation?) of many intellectual women. To examine the world is also, of course, the work of an artist. And "(even if jokes change nothing)," as Eve adds, one nevertheless sees and speaks and laughs and goes on—perseverance as essential to an *ars poetica* as to the life spirit of Enid Dame. Eve is forever intrigued by the snake; thus we learn that intelligence is a primal force, male and female, both. So is humor. Here we have it with a woman's sharp wit, and woman's powerful laughter. Who has celebrated these qualities so deliciously before?

"The Family on the Boat, a meditation in 3 parts" also speaks for the contemporary artist:

> We had brains dreams energy
> arrogance enough
> to believe we contained the world
> as the Ark contained us.

And so they were saved. In a toast to her parents, Noah's daughter thanks them for their wisdom: "'We are the children/ who came through the Flood alive/ and went on to do other things.'" And so does Enid survive, for us, in her words, in her profound wit; and— if "Arks" will be built, and if we can receive the wisdom given—so do we.

3.

Stone Shekhina is informed by scholarship, as well as by Dame's life of political involvement and her sharp views. Years ago, Dame became a student of Jewish myths and traditions; her work is rooted in her midrashic interpretation of Biblical texts. Mystic commentators and modern historians—such as Raphael Patai and Elaine Pagels—are also her sources.

At the same time, she became expert in craft: her language is precise, she captures nuance and inflection; her lines move in a unique "music of (her own) ordinary speech." And she is the master of many open and closed forms, notably the sestina. Hearing Enid read was always a rich surprise: her jubilant amusement sang through. One can "hear" her on the page, in her earlier, more confessional work, then in the persona poems of the Lilith series, and throughout *Stone Shekhina,* the most recent collection.

88

Noah's Ark is the center of this book, and laughter is its leit-motif. Sarah reports on her conversation with the Angel who announced her coming pregnancy: in "Sarah and the Angel" she says, "Laughter sprang out of me/ like water escaping a faucet/ or steam in a boiling pot! Wriggling its lid off./ I choked, 'Me, a mother? my good man,/ I'm 90 years old./ Don't be ridiculous.' " The angel chides her for giggling. She explains her life of hardships and ironies—hypocritical parents and a husband "who speaks to a God...who makes nothing easy for us." With a funny aside about how she frustrated the King of Egypt...whose "royal member withdrew/ then went hard as an eggplant." Sarah concludes, "So now we are old my lover/ is too weak to enter me/ (with his fine new circumcised penis)./ I am too dry to receive him..." and compares their bodies to dried fruits. In the peak of this conversation about her pregnancy, Sarah asks the young angel (in a shtetl inflection), "`What's wrong?/ You couldn't find anyone else?'" She finally makes the Angel laugh, and feels triumphant: "Our boundaries dissolved," Sarah declares, just as Enid dissolves boundaries between past and present, myth and reality, the powerful and the humble. "And I felt the power surge through me,/ a Jewish comedienne/ finding her audience!" The Angel chides her again for laughing. "I pulled myself upright. 'No/ My life is no joke./ But jokes help me live it.'" Midrashic inventions are the substance in much of Dame's work. Vivid personae are its flesh. Sophisticated linguistic form is its medium. And laughter is its key.

Dame's genius shows clearly in how she merges legendary and contemporary references. Noah's daughter appears again, after history has moved forward and Noah has become a souvenir-shop legend: "I want to shout,/ 'This isn't my father!/ He wasn't a blue-eyed saint.../ He didn't wear a neat bathrobe/ or mystical smile./ He was a small angry man...'" and time becomes "today":

> Today, after years
> of dry silence

I want to tell his story…
I want to release a memory
clear and fierce as a flame
or a bird over falling waters
of this father who built a boat
around the unruly world
and carried it off to safety
not for business or pleasure
or entrance to heaven.
Because it had to be done.
Because it was what he could do.

(from "Free-Lance World Saver")

The poet speaking as Noah's daughter preserves this practical, realistic figure of a man, yes, but the extended metaphor incorporates something of a father we might have all wished for, a man who might have lived in our "real" times. There are more glimpses of such a father in Enid's earlier work; and the men we dream of—would that they could build "a boat/ around this unruly world." The poem moves so deeply that a reader finds herself wanting to believe that my father also did what "had to be done," and my forefathers, and now, who? Who will "carry (this world) off to safety." Through the simple old story, opened and re-constituted here, Dame raised the most complex questions of our lives, because she loved the terrible world. And the animals and the people in it.

What would Enid Dame be thinking and feeling this year? What would she have been writing about these continuing wars? The 2008 election? This new American presidency? I reread her many-layered poems and wonder. How we miss her wisdom, her voice, her love.

4.

There is an ironic vein in Dame's work—embedded in historic paradox. Laughter connects grief and survival. In "Sarah: The Place Beyond Laughter," the great poem on bitter endurance, Dame teaches the uses of laughter. Here, in a special version of pre-history, Sarah speaks in a modern voice: "I made two kings laugh./ They didn't walk off in a huff./ They didn't reach for their weapons" and "Like a blind woman relying/ on her nimble, seeing fingers,/ I felt my way around a world/ ruled first by my father's gods…/ then by my husband's invisible Voice…" Protest enters Sarah's meditations: "But now, husband, you've brought us to a place/ where words turn to stones,/ and laughter turns poison…" Isaac—whose name means "laughter" (I learned from Enid)—is brought to the rock by his father. It happens suddenly in the poem, as in the world such an event always does; and the poem speaks for what is seen: "A knife deflects light…" Then the poet comments from her contemporary vantage point: "Maybe some other beings/ observing from the bleachers/ somewhere out among the cooling stars/ would find this amusing." But then Dame speaks as the mother in that terribly familiar story: "I try to heal/ the stunned boy you brought home/ with words I don't believe in…/ How can I live with you now?" The murderous patriarch, in the name of his faith, has brought the woman to a place where "The earth is drained of quick blood." It is "a place beyond laughter." Dame has always taken us forward into our frightening present, by moving, laughing, praying, digging deep into the past.

This poem is what I chose to read, before Enid's death, at an anti-war reading in Morristown, NJ, not far from George Washington's headquarters. Enid was thrilled to learn what a powerful meaning her work has in our time. She had participated in many such rallies, over decades, but she was so modest, she didn't always know that she was saying, as a great writer, exactly what we needed.

Enid has been known for her midrashic work, but she has also been expert at satire, as in whimsical characterizations of personae in "Jerusalem Syndrome" (based on actual cases), people who imagine themselves as ancient figures, but whom the poet saw with modernized quirks. She could be mordant

91

too, her satire leveled at contemporary behavior while finding amusement in Biblical figures.

By the time she had gathered her women (and men) to emerge under the blessings of the Shekhina, Lilith, the daring, sexy woman from patriarchal folklore who declared that she had "kicked myself out of paradise…" had already become Enid's model. Enid also identified with Eve, with Noah's daughter, with Sarah…She was confronting sexism in religion…as in "All Grandmother's stories/ were turned into stone. Something was trapped in translation." And she liberated the truth (as we come to believe it)! In the final poem in *Stone Shekhina* Dame talks directly to Lilith: "Lilith, I don't cut my grass/ as you never cut your hair./ I picture you in my backyard/ where it's always cool and ferny,/…where wild berries tangle/…Lilith, you smell like the earth and marigolds and mulchy leaves…" Here is a celebration of earth from an earthy and loving woman, a real sensualist, who was also a bold critic of convention.

Dame had surely found her garden, "Where roses sag and break their waters…/ you dip your toes in green mud." She rejected the power mower that neighbors wanted to buy her: "…How can I tell them I'm terrified of power?/ There's too much let loose in the world./ It's one gift I don't need." And with a little joke on the Messiah, who will come as another form of authority—"…carrying a squirtgun filled with chemicals…" the poem ends by asking Lilith to "bless this garden/ while both of us/ still use it." Like her gutsy Lilith, Enid Dame knew how to see (and resist) the evils of power in this world, and how to bless.

5.

We will always miss our great-hearted friend, this poet who moved so purely against canonical imperatives and against human cruelty, but never preaching. The poems will keep us steady—intelligent, awake, tempered with Enid's healthy skepticism, and with the sympathetic laughter of recognition. Enid's personality shines through, modestly yet surely. And she is smiling broadly, as she did whenever she was giving a reading of her marvelous poems.

16. There Is Nothing Like an Enid Dame
by Martin Tucker

Love bears no grief except when unfulfilled. Yet grief bares all of love fulfilled, and lost. Enid Dame's letters to Donald Lev (in *Where Is the Woman?*) are full of such naked love without one article of clothing of regret. Such love showered Donald into the rain of happiness and later the storm of grief and still later into the presence of renewable memory of gratitude. Even if Enid's poems were not remarkable kernels of joyous acceptance of life's contraries and thus the golden coins of a reader's fortune, her letters, as printed in *Where Is the Woman?*, would claim for her a position in an epistolary pantheon. Yet her greatest claim is as a poet of the underworld of wit and restorative self-mockery. A reader cannot leave her work without a smile at the geography of foibles she explores. She is like a visitor walking into a colony ruled by habitual confusion and taking notes on everything and finally joining in the fun even as she relates to the appeal without any passport of rationalization. Consider "Persephone" (in *Anything You Don't See*), in which the mythic goddess of Grecian lore becomes the modern girl dragged into an underground of sexual abuse. Even though the pederast, who smells of "old clothes" and rocks "like a leaky old boat" and who "shipwrecks inside" her, and even though the girl calls him "Mama" when he fondles her, there is a sense of wistful survival, of unconquerable inviolation. Enid's Persephone makes of subjection not merely an experience to be suffered but one to gain something by.

Enid's references are less to classical Greek sources than to her uniquely biblical ones. What she does with Eve, and particularly with her well-known chapbook on Lilith (*Lilith and Her Demons*), is extraordinary. In Enid's hands Eve becomes more than an outsourcing for the history of women—she shapes into a loving, eccentric, contradictory figure of lust and love. So full of quirky, sly humor, Enid's poems are as forgiving of transgression as a wide-ranged strainer of tea

94

leaves. She refreshes by her compassionate nature, but she is not merely good-natured. Her poetry is that rare container of innocence and natural sophistication, the paradox of the untutored wise street-cracker. In the titular poem that opens *Anything You Don't See*, Eve loves Adam but knows marriage, once outside Paradise Garden (somewhere probably in Brooklyn), has burdens of recrimination. Though she does not explicitly ask Adam if he married her out of guilt, the question remains in the air (and in the heirs of their union). The question is suggested in the poem's final couplet: "He never will/ forgive me."

Perhaps nothing characterizes Enid's sense of slyly good humor as her Lilith poems. These poems express a core of her body of work—the sense of recognition that no matter what home Lilith inhabits, she will always be granted the status of a familiar outsider. The recognition comes to Lilith with some pain but also with a note of some other gratuity—experience, as any long-suffering Jewish woman (and man) knows, is a bread of woe that may be buttered for wisdom.

Writers writing about someone else are, as the truism goes, writing about themselves under an alias. In her Lilith and her Eve poems (she has one particularly juicy poem about Eve and Lilith meeting in the produce department of a supermarket and comparing silently their notes on Adam), Enid suggests how healthy both misbehavior and occasional sinning can be. Of course she recognizes the limits of crossing such borders, and the dangers that such crossings present. Lilith claims she is fine (after all, she lives now with her taxicab mate in New Jersey, in "Lilith"), but something is churning in her to get going again into the challenge of struggling excitement. Eve writes home (if a poem may be called a home, a shelter) that her husband Adam's snores are as comforting as a radiator's steam, and as any immigrant who has lived in a cold-water tenement flat knows, that is a comfort to be desired. Enid always posits that Lilith and Eve know—indeed proclaim—they are exiles in promised lands.

Lilith knows that the names she's been called for 4,000 years won't stop growing though they remain the same names. In the initial poem in the Lilith chapbook, Enid has Lilith sum up her permanently transient life:

> sometimes
> I cry in the bathroom
> remembering Eden
> and the man and the god
> I couldn't live with

Enid's poems—and her spirit—will survive because her words are those of the exile singing not in the wilderness but in the community of fellowship of outsiders and in the indestructible humor of survival. The feeling is communicated in one of her last poems as a house ("The Idea of a House" in *Where Is the Woman?*). Here are her words:

> The idea of a house
> will persist
> even when the house is sold
> even when the lives lived there
> live elsewhere
> and newcomers move in.
> They will unpack new words vegetables
> cooking pots.
> They will remodel the kitchen.
> They will add another chapter
> to the house's biography.

Appendix 1

a selection of Enid's poems

Chagall Exhibit, 1996

If you want your sky to turn red,
you'll have to get out of Vitebsk,
go to St. Petersburg, go to Paris,
go to High Falls, New York,
learn someone else's mountains,
learn how light strides down the streets whose names you
don't know yet,
how it stakes out its claim.

He sits in a window in Paris,
man faced cat on the sill,
painting the sky red in his remembered village.
Last year, when he lived there, it was all green,
eerie chartreuse over muddy earth houses.
In that light, people were ill lit.
They moved through their somber routines,
sweeping the streets renewing the dead man's candles,
slowly as planets trudging their orbits.
He etched in their faces carefully, a good student,
faceted faces like diamonds.
No wonder the picture won a prize!

In the memory, which he eagerly paints
dazzled on conversation   poetry   coffee,
the sky explodes   houses shimmer   the dead man
is becoming someone else.
But faces are washed of their features,
blank as sand banks.

Everything surges out of proportion,
even the facts:
the uncle eating carrots on the rooftop,
the lovers' sweet meetings   the holy man dipping snuff.

Even the jokes tilt wildly:
the rabbi's extra soul performs somersaults,
the men stoop like question marks,
the milkmaid flitters among stars.

You can go back, he went back, but it won't be the same.
You'll be the bridegroom triumphant in modern clothes,
the modern parent displaying the well equipped baby,
the visitor at the house of the dead fathers.
Already, the mother's stove is starting to swell like a bread
loaf.
Already, the houses are starting to tilt.

When you go back again, later, it will be gone.
No village   no mud   no roof sitting uncle   no carroty
kitchen.
You walk through a modern city
and the pictures that weigh down your suitcase
aren't photographs.

Landsman   neighbor   historian: your village doesn't
exist,
except on the walls of the Jewish Museum, which we visit
today
stamped with our paper circles: bringing our notebooks,
our knowing comments   our several languages
we tramp through your muddy streets
watch your sky turn delirious
get your jokes note resemblances
between our uncles and yours,
as if we had always lived here,
as if we had seen it first.

Mike Gold and the Classics

"O Lorenzo
...I would end this strife,
Become a Christian, and thy loving wife."

Shylock's daughter, Jessica,
in *The Merchant of Venice*

1. In this version, Jessica is the villain.
This is a tale of a Jewish father betrayed.
This play's a classic. We tore it up like a coat
restitched it, making it over to fit our story.
(We come from a long line of tailors.
We understand alterations.)

2. All the seats were filled that night in the Yiddish theater.
(Shakespeare often sold out on the Lower East Side.)
The air was heavy with clouds of smoky emotion.
On stage, a Jewish father was the hero.
A battered, self pitying hero. A hero who loses.
(An old woman in the front row sighed, "It's just like life.")

My father's favorite author sat as a boy
and wept in the dark at the bad daughter's treachery.
Beguiled by the gentile world, she ran down the fire escape,
bearing her father's bloody heart in a bag.
(Somewhere uptown her sexy *shaygetz* waited,
smoking a Lucky, reading a dime novel.)
"I'm an American!" Jessica proudly asserted.
"That's what you think," the audience muttered darkly.

The future author and revolutionist sniffled.
He wanted to follow Jessica down those stairs.
He wanted to sit in his mother's kitchen forever.
He wanted to join Buffalo Bill's Wild West Show.
He wanted to write great poems in American lingo.
He wanted to blaze like a star! But what would he do with his family?

3. When I read that play, back in World Literature I,
I thought was Portia. All the Jewish girls did.
When I ran away from my father, after I graduated,
psychologists cheered me on! Talk show hosts said, "Atta girl!"
Families are old coats. You have to shake them off.
You don't stay at home in America. You go somewhere else.
This is a country of passionate self creators.
Jessica knew this. Shylock wouldn't admit it.

4. When I left my father, I ran away down the mountain.
It was fall. The world had turned orange. The roses had died.
I rented a tenement room in the glittering city.
Each day on my way to work I passed the theater
where my father's favorite author had his epiphany.
(The building was dark, but the marquee proclaimed
the last play, *The Bride Got Farblondget.*)

I married two gentiles. But now, I live with a Jew.
I brought him back here, back here to these flowering mountains.
Outside, the orange leaves fall. Our last rose is red and arrogant.
We drink valpolicella and light candles for our dead.
(All of our fathers are dead. We buy lots of candles.)

5. My father's favorite author disappeared into a footnote.
His brave assumed name glitters like polished coins.
His real name was shoved in a pocket, an old passport.
His politics did him in or was it his dream of America?
My father met him once; he never forgot it.
He shook his hand. He said he preferred him to Hemingway.

Lilith, I Don't Cut My Grass

> ...although Lilith has existed since the sixth, or even
> the fifth day of Creation, she is not immortal.
>
> —Raphael Patai
> *The Hebrew Goddess*

Lilith, I don't cut my grass
as you never cut your hair.
I picture you in my backyard
where it's always cool and ferny,
where jewelweeds grow taller than trees,
where wild berries tangle
like knots in cats' fur.

I see you sorting out the birds from the cats:
two of your favorite animals.
Contradictions never scared you.

Lilith, you smell like the earth
and marigolds and mulchy leaves.
Your arms are mud-bespattered.
You don't look like my mother.

I couldn't ask my mother
for a blessing.
She was too much afraid
of her own craziness.
She only spoke to cats.

Every few months
she went to an expert
to burn all the wilderness
out of her hair.

Once she tried to take me with her.
I scratched and fought,

yowled, ran up an elm tree.
It took years to climb down.

Lilith, I'm almost 50.
I'm running out of time, money, eyesight.
I still bleed but for how long?
Not like this yard where everything is liquid:
where roses sag and break their waters,
tomatoes offer up their juices,
slugs die dreamily in beerbowls,
you dip your toes in green mud.

Lilith, neighbors are complaining.
They're-collecting money
to buy me a power mower.
How can I tell them
I'm terrified of power?
There's too much let loose in the world.
It's one gift I don't need.

Lilith, it's growing later.
I know you won't hang on forever.
They say Messiah's coming any day now.
I hear his footsteps ringing in the hallway.
The clean clang of authority.
I see his shadow looming
big as a condominium
sucking up the sun.
No stopping that man!
He's carrying a squirtgun filled with chemicals.
No room for weeds in his world.

Lilith, bless this garden
while both of us
still use it.

The Woman Who was Water

The woman who was water
lived on the edges of rooms,
knew when to withdraw.

The woman who was water
came to Brooklyn,
and filled every basement.

The woman who was water
left all of her lovers
clean.

The woman who was water
insisted no one understood her,
saw herself gentle as mist,

a rain-pearly morning, a sweet lilac fog.
So, when she battered at shingles,
gnawed through foundations,

burst out of pipes,
she knew she was offering love.
Why didn't people want it?

The woman who was water
was not analytical.
She knew three things:

They couldn't pass laws against her.
They couldn't declare her harmless.
They couldn't exist without her.

The woman who was water
could power a city,
or drown it.

Appendix 2

a selection of poems to Enid

Russian Snow in Brooklyn

for Enid Dame

Don't read Dostoevsky in Brooklyn
not when you're seventeen
not when you're seventy
you wake up and it's snowing
even the vacant lots look virgin
you can hardly see the streets
for the snow blinding snow
a lone Siberian tiger begs for mercy

Next door you hear deep voices
Russian voices
they're getting deeper
so is the snow
the news from Moscow is no good
there's a run on the banks
and not a single ruble in my pocket

Next door they're hatching Cyrillic conspiracies
next door they're blackmailing my sleep
next door they're practicing Russian roulette
I close my eyes
hoping to be rescued
by an American fire truck
with bells and sirens blaring
a big red hook and ladder
the color of the revolution
that never happens
for all the revolutionaries in Brooklyn
and all the revolutionary fires

In the burned out vacant lot next door
empty vodka bottles chill
beneath deep White Russian drifts
a dumped refrigerator stands out
colder than ever

waiting for salvation
waiting to swallow a child
on New Year's morning

David Gershator

Poetry Teacher

Reading into their work
a potential visible
to none but their creator
she made them feel worthy.

They changed pebbles to pearls
she said
Was this love or blindness?
Did she believe it?

Roberta Gould

Bat Mitzvah—Portion Noah

The drowned souls

when the springs roared up
the floods through the riven abyss
then opened as well
all the windows of heaven.

The drowned children

no foothold below
and the throat choking waters
and all the drowned mothers
inhaling the water
though it might have been gas.

Then died every life that had
breath in its nostrils excepting
that silent, good man
who walked with his God.

So she stood in the pulpit this thirteen year old
contending with God
as had Jacob and Moses
this covenant's daughter
and she asked, no, demanded
to know who was just
though he call up the dawn
and show morning its place.

So wrapped in that shawl—
the shawl of the drowned
woven five fathers back

spoke of seed time and harvest
the unfinished God
the wind, the dove,
and the sprig of olive.

Walter Hess

This poem, originally created for our granddaughter on the occasion of her Bat Mitzvah, seems to me equally fitting as a tribute to Enid Dame, especially after rereading *Lilith & Her Demons*. What suggested this re-dedication was my memory of the challenging and questioning of God's justice by our granddaughter Stephanie in her Bat Mitzvah speech. That stance which might have been the height of chutzpah some time ago, was validated by all the Enid Dames of the last several decades. Stephanie, then at thirteen, knew her power and her capacity better because of them. She is, I feel, a legatee of Enid Dame.

A Little Something—for Enid

Angry chefs are writing poems
The poets are making chicken soup, tasty tasty
The firemen are setting fires and the firewomen are firing
      the firemen
"if that's your job you don't have job no more!"
The Cedars of Tavermon are busy swaying and shading the
      gravesite
And the rocks are growing
So quickly the only job is filing down their fingernails
With electric drills and cheese graters (you get to wear headphones

Luckily homeless people want to read my poems
I stand at the newsstand making mouth moves "I can't stand it!" noise-
lessly
Maybe all I'm saying is it's a real job, being unemployed

It's not on TV
Not even on the radio
It's not in *Books in Print* or *Out of Print* or *Digital Books*
      Could care less for Print
You cannot skywrite it from a bipolarplane, spray paint on a dijirrigible
Your mother rocked you to sleep with it, that's all
And you didn't even know it because you fell asleep and the words
      sailed clouds
In starry water over blue sandcastled grassy grassy hills

Animals can talk, they are movie stars. And war.
War is forgotten. What was war? says the pug to the poodle
As they nosh on a noodle pudding
Served by Enid Dame who has a real job,
Cue Lility, the banjo canter.
A job here on earth, no tips allowed.
Enid this chicken soup is for you
To give away, too.

Bob Holman

Enid

Your picture hangs above my desk
Face radiant, smile serene.

I would not be surprised if tears
Tumbled from beneath those Buddha lids
Or blood sprang from the outstretched palm,
Given world events.

The other night, I heard a rustling
And waited for a ghostly visit.
I need to canonize my dead,
Receive their blessing.

Patron of poets
Your presence grows in absence,
Your words an eternal flame
A torch to light dark corners.

Legends could be spun.
You could not save the world
But your words saved souls
And will again.

Judith Lechner

Poem for Enid Dame

yet another snow frosts
fresh green ivy and new tubers
pushing their way through frozen dirt

this is new York city in march
with brown wind and bits of filthy
plastic bags flying from leafless trees
in a bitter display
it's the damp brooding
of too many good people
now swimming in a moon tide
diving off of other dreams, the angels
their hair netting the universe

Ellen Aug Lytle

Epithalamion for Enid and Don

Enid Dame Tribute, Sunday, March 21, 2004, Cedar Tavern

I've always thought of Enid Dame and Donald Lev as the heart and soul of the Village poetry scene and, in an ideal sense, the poetry scene in New York. Their styles are as distinctive as their devotion was seamless. They expressed their integrity, humor, and commitment in causes and celebrations we could share. Through the pages of Home Planet News we could walk around and be ourselves. They brought us into community.

For their wedding in 1994, celebrated at the Cedar Tavern, I wrote a kind of epithalamion. It contains a brief medley of their words.

Keeping our home planet on course, you steer toward
Lilith and Brooklyn and ordinary people
turning into Rita Hayworth on park benches,
mothers as revolutionaries,
the Rosenbergs, lost causes and poets
and making chicken soup in a ghetto.
You question what's easy,
because "anything you don't see
will come back to haunt you."
You advise, "Do not feed the assumptions."
Your "peculiar merriment" rides
a righteous anger.

You learned how to marry your work
and each other
distinctly.

I think you got it right from the beginning,
right from the beginning.

> *D. H. Melhem*

You Enid Dame with Your Cloud of Beautiful Hair and Your Kindness

Lover of large books, old Old Testaments, dusted-off apocrypha.
In thrall to grandmother stories, witch and angel tales,
the fierce growls of goddesses, to rebels' voices,
to the makers of soup.

Good friend to Lilith, to Lot's wife Idith. You introduced us,
called her by name—and Naamah, Noah's wife.
You welcomed Hagar and the wronged Dina
with her few calm years at the end.
Eve visited often.

Not only women came.
You listened to Noah's crazed ideas, to Japeth's horror
as the ark rose with the waters and he heard the cries of the drowning
and to Shem and his vision:
houses turned into arks, soup ladle oars, many more saved—
what could have been.

You had them to tea, for wine
and outside one of your windows the jewelweed grew tall,
its orange petals winking
and the Rose of Sharon dropped its damp blossoms
as the summer deepened. Outside another
the sea murmured and the Russian shopkeepers, too
and the D train grumbled along the tracks.
The Shekhinah's hand lay lightly around your shoulders
and your voice stayed sure.

And we came, too
to listen in. No one was turned away.
Come in, you said, smiling—*New friends for you,*
new mothers, fathers.
Let me tell you what I know.
Bring your notebooks. Write the stories down.
Imagine what happens next.

Constance Norgren

For Enid Dame

Enid Dame, friendly spirit,
no longer walks with a happy smile
down the bus aisle holding bouquets
                    of dried summer flowers
to take back to Brooklyn

Enid Dame, friendly spirit,
no longer grates fresh ginger for tea
                    in High Falls
when we stop by to drop off bundles of the Woodstock
Journal

Enid Dame, friendly spirit
no longer charts her beautiful lines
with her startling voice

Enid Dame, friendly spirit,
is freed from the tyranny of the microphone

Enid Dame, friendly spirit
no longer travels for treatment to California
no longer waits for the multilith to be fixed
no longer takes the tube
        beneath the Trade Center to teach in New Jersey
nor flies to Michigan in her final weeks to read
        poetry at a benefit for Bridges
nor reads again for the seniors at the Workman's Circle

Enid Dame, friendly Spirit
is freed from grading papers sick and weaken'd
just to have a trace of dignity
in a capitalist slavocracy

Enid Dame, friendly spirit
No longer studies how the Shekinah
As a divine feminine entity is
"prompted by her compassionate nature
to argue with God in defense of man"

Or maybe she does

Enid Dame, friendly
Spirit no longer signs her book to my wife and me
"Two wonderful people! May the Shekinah
shine on everything you do!"

Boats full of poets drift across the Universe
It's as simple as that

and maybe she'll seek a realignment
in the chains of justice

Enid Dame, friendly spirit
shining now in her stories & words

Edward Sanders

Written on the way to her funeral in Brighton Beach 12-29-03
and on the morning of her memorial in Woodstock 2-14-04.

121

A Cup for Enid

The floor falls away from our feet.
Light fixtures installed in the ceiling
are overcome by stars.

I put a cup out for Enid, late to the reading,
and leave the door open.
It is almost five years, but the wine keeps sweet.

I try to prepare my boyfriend for what she is like,
her voice not husky or smooth, not like a milkshake.
Her voice is like a surprise, inflected see-saw of words

taking you to Brooklyn, to Beaver Falls,
to a row of tulips, unbridled bulbs waiting also.
I try to tell him how she overwhelms me

with her art, her poet's soul that puts
her take on life so cleanly down that I can
taste her mother's chicken soup,

see the candles glow with Sabbath revery,
hear the scratch of her pen transforming
paper to gold. It is hard to explain.

You had to be there.
The door is open, but only a breeze blows in.
The wine sinks lower in the cup.

Cheryl A. Rice

Lilith Mourns

(in memory of Enid Dame)

I returned. I always do. And in returning—
Adam a memory distant but strong—I made
friends. There's the danger: friends.

They take a toll, dying. They are not
like infants, though I do mourn mine. This one
welcomed me, sang my songs, brought me

to life in her poems. There were so many
hours we spent together it became almost as if
she shared my mind. I could call her sister

and not be off the mark, though she was not there
in the beginning. And now she has gone
from my side, will not add more to my story.

And knowing there are others who will is no solace.
It is her voice I miss, not theirs. She was the one
who listened and spoke. She was the one I call *friend.*

Matthew J. Spireng

For Enid Dame, Poet

I

She was a stranger, and a friend.
Cat lover, to the end like a cat-
Somewhat secretive and self-contained
Too proud to tell to all dismayed-
A creature of, and not of, our ways.

She disliked technology, but sought out knowledge
all the secret corners of the heart were hers;
l heard her teach a class once
and with almost witch-like intuition
brought the students out to a vision of poetry
or the text of a story, not just what happened next,
but the pith, the meaning. She warmed them,
bringing back the feeling other classes had numbed.

She, childless, a decision for poetry, could brood
like a mother hen, clucking over the papers, an A/ a C-
or, clutching the large black handbag
of her rectitude like a doctor would go to tutor
or proctor an exam. She made the students open their minds,
and her colleagues too, though she had scant time to talk.

If there was something odd about her pose,
it was her almost unbelievable purity—
never to speak an unkind word of anyone—
championing the weak—an ill-formed angel
in shabby clothes, a saint, which she sort of was,

trying, in the last days, to finish her grades,
protesting the occupation of the West Bank,
which she found an outrage...Skin and bone
and graying skin, when she came back
in September, maybe all that goodness

had suppressed the antidotes to cancer,
or maybe cancer doesn't care a hoot `
about goodness or melancholy
but she who had praised life decided
to carry on without telling anyone
and so we now pay her—more than her salary—

tribute with devotion I have never seen,
for the sick queen in flowered garments
from a secondhand shop in Brooklyn or Queens,
you wouldn't know she'd ever been in Manhattan.
Bloomingdale's or the Soho scene didn't exist
as far as she was concerned. And she wore
her doctorate with so little stiffness,
her knowledge supple with humane interest.

She loved Brooklyn, said her husband,
himself a kind of rusty pump like the one
from their place in High Falls
where they spent much time, a falling down shanty,
but a kind of shrine outside of work
outside of time where the long grasses grew
uncut and through her kitchen window
on a good night Lilith or the Shekinah peaked through
came to visit, to drink a coffee.

II

So many poets, so many books.
Will her words, compassionate and bold,
continue to mediate between
the seen and the unseen?
Comrades in words, colleagues and friends,

gather to oppose the force of death.
Not like the stone ashteroths
she wrote about. The path of poetry
is strewn by a storm of paper;
litter no one about.

She left no heirs
though something may survive
like Chiddiock Tichbourne's elegy,
with no one to tend to the graveside,
the almost famous alongside the unknown.
But these poems, like the memory of sunshine,
Of moonlight, ring changes in us;
As Pasternak wrote, and the same holds for poems:
"To live a life is not to cross a field."

Nikki Stiller

Enid Dame

Enid Dame
everything is important—
your words
    tell me not to grieve   but to carve
a fierce and tender goodness

from the Hudson River breeze
sweep the chipped pieces of my hours here
past the threshold of just myself
let them bloom outside   as you did

even in the darkest air
anything you don't see
will come back to haunt you
you wrote   vegetable stands   Bronx walk-ups

a mezuzah   gooseberry jam   Brooklyn rooftops
subway riders scrawling pen marks on their hands
Jews and leftists   dishes   a Brighton Beach boardwalk
where old socialists played chess

immigrants   radicals   exiles   partisans   second-hand
shops
people with numbers stitched on their arms
I pace my floor as if it were time
I could scuff and wear away

I peel frailty
    from myself like layers of an onion
the spider won't stop weaving
in my mind where sometimes I forget

there are also apricots   basil   thyme
and someone always pours tea into a glass cup
you borrowed the lips of biblical woman
you knocked on their spirits palpable as plaster

and they needed you to listen
to speak them to us   translate
listen
to the world you generously release

to those who read you
it is not at home with itself yet
still hungers
when I can't inhabit faith

want memory to dissolve
nouns and minutes
that are wounded
want life to be a cradle

comfort me bone by bone god's lioness

Yerra Sugarman

Sestinas of the City "Cluttered with Roses"

(Almost) a book of sestinas, *Anything*
You Don't See comes from Enid Dame's
mastery of rich content in a form
that seduces her vision to wander in and out
of her past, Brooklyn,
layers of states she has and hasn't left.

The gap folk history left
open, Biblical lacunae, and anything
necessary to the worlds of truth, Dame's
pen has been filling, with womanly form,
impressions of her father's Bronx, The Bridge, and Brooklyn
today, hers, a richness she can't speak without

praising—even while protesting about
evictions, stray lives, conditions her mother left
for her to understand, unravel, and re-form,
with irony binding life and poetry like anything
seen from a taxi mirror in Brooklyn:
living and writing merge reflectively in Dame's

retrospective pieces. Enid Dame is
capable of conjuring historic women, formal
figures like Eve or Lilith, stronger now they're out
of HIStory, revisioned, but she has never left
her personal life in shadow: Enid's Brooklyn
poems are peopled with parents/Zionists, immigrants, anything

she culls from memory to color hope. Anything
goes, but it's made to fit: The form
acquires dialogue, with idiom, and images never without
the sense of ancestors who, living and dying, left
her with remnants of a world—Dame's
legacy—of penny arcade and "dogeared lake": Brooklyn

becomes cosmos and philosophy—of Brooklyn
boundary and depth: the sea, the "El," shops, anything
of notice, even the decrepit rich in detail, Dame's
collection: machines, games, Mickey Mouse, leftover
buttons, kisses, noises, wise cats; ranging about
New York, and back to the Diaspora, the lines inform

Anything You Don't See, honoring Enid Dame's
parents: Vision is left to her, now steeped in Brooklyn
idiom, her songs about loving a community fit the form.

Madeline Tiger

130

Enid

You did a great service
plunging us through the brick wall
of the patriarchs
to show the sweet funny
sensible woman's point of view.
You did it without rancor or raising your voice,
a feat i have yet to master.
You made it easier to accept those bastards
with their bony shoulders under blankets at 2 a.m.,
that pinched look about the nose and chin.
Even god had bunions.

You took us for a little walk around the neighborhood,
like Henry Miller, showing us
inside certain windows, embracing humanity
like the arms of Meridel LeSueur
across the prairie, across borders,
across the ravages of this cruel century's night.
There has always been a star,
a pearl of laughter, a broken dish
and, us guffawing at our ultimate ridiculousness.
In a mammalian world peremptory orders—
unless it's *Don't jump! We love you!*—
are out of place.

Under the pitiless warmonger's sun
on our hills and valleys, then 'til now—
guns in the airports,
smirking Napoleon in the oval office,

bombs on our beautiful ancient cities—
we need shade trees, we need laughter
and running water to bring us from field to field.
I can hear your high voice in the corner
making sure no one has been left out.
I can hear you as this paper sails across
the bedroom floor:
that's about it. go back to sleep.

Janine Pommy Vega

Sparkle Like Diamonds, A Review

Stone Shekhina: Poems by Enid Dame
(A Three Mile Harbor Book)

Enid makes me believe in
All I believe in
Swell a heart so full
Tears sparkle like diamonds
Like her words

"…I'm real as this windowwall bottle
holding a piece of the sky
lightly, between its walls."

Enid igniting imagination
I become bubble in this
Mouth blown bottle, with
Light fractured angles
Her words let me be a
Rainbow

"…The world, after all,
was created from pieces of alphabet,
And if God can zbe a great poet,
You can be Dr. Seuss."

Enid freeing all this laughter as
She scours the bible in
Search of our soul

Lilith, Eve, Miriam, Esther
Did we know of Noah's daughter?
There, at the ready, to answer
Questions no one in the patriarchal
Tomb thought to ask.

"How were the animals fed?
By all of us—but mostly Mother
I see her in the tiny, sweaty kitchen
Chopping up pieces of seaweed,

Making soup out of salt water and discarded shells.
(Meal was forbidden, of course)...
A red parrot perched on her shoulder;
I sat on the floor, absorbed,
Feeding seaweed scraps to the goat."

Enid tempting and seducing me
With the creatures that inhabit my
Cerebellum—living transparency
On my lens,
Burnt tree seats to sage monkeys
Sayir_____ amen to the Enid truthsayer;

Review wants to write out every
Poem word...
Say, read, breathe, become homage
Sound.
I was the boy on the boat
the youngest son still a teenager
recently married to a sharp-edged girl
(her bones poked me at night in unexpected places)
She thought this was an adventure.

I felt sorry for the bodies
I saw floating past like rubber bathtub toys
Pop said, 'They were stupid, improvident.'
I muttered, 'This sucks! It isn't right."

Be praise to secrets spoken,
The tender become the tortured
Become prizes, trophies
Boy become man, Enid
Sees, Enid tells;

She names the survived; the familiar
Seeds with their sons and sons' sons
And also the silent daughters,
We become privy to their conversation
With God and Angels;

Life was hard inside domesticity
Children of survivors, children of
A plan; in all this my mind

Recalls we are survivors of God
Of God's plan too;

Enid lets Noah's daughter testify
"To the children of Noah and Naamah
We have survived the worst God could do to the world.
We have survived our parents'
most radiant plans and wretched failures.
We have survived their love
which sometimes beat down like a storm
And sometimes withdrew like a lake in a desert.
We have survived the rainbows of their ecstasies
the ocean bottom of their self-destruction
the bumpy landing on the mountain top.

We have survived
growing up.

We have taken their wisdom,
as much as we could use.
We thank them for it.

We are the children
who came through the Flood alive
And went on to do other things."

Enid has done Stone Shekhina
Words carrying cadence & sound
Beauty and meaning, words to
Feed off and be nourished by
I am full; I give thanks.

Carletta Joy Walker

Without Tears for Enid

No grave looks around the table
no sad faces at the tributes

Lilith
…from the Assyrian—Babylonian,
Lilitu, "belonging to the night"
first wife of Adam,
a character…
"night hag"
"screech owl"

Halevai!

Enid freed the screech
and grew a voice to humanize
harmonize the myth
sing it to the moment's current.

Enid
of the midrash line—full-blooded,
belonging to the light,
blazing wife of Donald,
a character…
illuminating
in flight

Barry Wallenstein

Appendix 3

Two essays by Enid Dame

"I May Be a Bit of a Jew": What Contemporary Jewish American Poets Learned from Allen Ginsberg and Sylvia Plath by Enid Dame

It is commonly believed that contemporary American poetry changed radically and permanently in 1955 at the Six Gallery in San Francisco, when a young Allen Ginsberg declaimed his new poem "Howl" to an enthusiastic audience, and thereby set off the San Francisco Poetry Renaissance. As Michael McClure described this event and its impact:

> We had gone beyond a point of no return—and we were ready for it. . None of us wanted to go back to the gray, chill, militaristic silence, to the intellective void—to the land without poetry—to the spiritual drabness. (Schumacher, 215)

In a seminal article which appeared in the *New York Times* a year later, Richard Eberhart characterized the poets of this movement (for so it had become) by saying, "They have exuberance and a young will to kick down the doors of elder consciousness and established practice"(Schumacher, 240).

A similar impact was felt, by a somewhat different poetry audience, upon the publication of Robert Lowell's *Life Studies* (1956). As A. Alvarez asserted, this book "appeared at the height of the tightlipped fifties, the era of doctrinaire New Criticism...and the whole elaborate, iron dogma by which poetry was separated utterly from the men (sic) who made it" (23). *Life Studies* replaced "impersonality" and "exquisitely dandified irony" with "immediacy" and "vulnerability" (24).

It would take many years, however, for either poetic movement to penetrate the thick walls of academia, behind which the New Critics were entrenched. As Adrienne Rich points out, at this time, "white and male middle-class poets were being hired into the universities as writing teachers, while university-trained scholars were replacing poets as the interpreters of poetry" (99). Aspiring student poets often lived double lives. In their own work and Creative Writing classes, poetry was a response to highly personal, even embarrassing feelings, situations and observations, often written in highly charged, or eccentric language; in their literature classes, poetry was abstract, abstruse, understated, ironic, and, above all, "universal." Yet the language, allusions, and underlying assumptions of the poetry that was being taught did suggest a particular context: one that was white, Anglo-Saxon, male, and middle (or upper) class. The young poet, especially if she were female, working-class, nonwhite, or non-gentile might well feel excluded from such a tradition. A Jewish student poet, for example, especially a woman, might find herself both stimulated and silenced by her literature courses, even when they were taught with passion by inspired professors. Given the cultural and intellectual atmosphere of the times, she might well be unsure how to respond as a poet. Should she, like the Beat poets evoked by Eberhart, kick the doors in, or knock politely and ask to be allowed to enter? And, once inside, would she know what language was required of her? Must she present herself as a person with no culture, no language, of her own? Should she impersonate a member of the dominant, non-Jewish society? Should she choose so abstract—love, justice—or so minutely specific—the way wet leaves look against the oddly vivid green of an October lawn—as to appear devoid of ethnicity?

Writing specifically of women poets, Alicia Ostriker speaks of a "submerged tradition" (15) running through their poetry over the years, only to emerge unequivocally in the 1960's. I suggest that a similar, parallel (and often overlapping) process can be identified in the body of Jewish-American poetry.*

*The poets associated with *Tree Magazine*, founded in 1967 by David Meltzer, combined Beat influence with a Jewish sensibility and knowledge of Kabbala.

The publication of *A Big Jewish Book* in 1978, in which editor Jerome Rothenberg presented contemporary translations of and modern responses to an alternative, mystical set of Jewish beliefs, signaled the fact that Jewish poets were searching for ways to express, and re-interpret, their Jewishness. This volume was followed by the near-comprehensive *Voices Within the Ark* (1982), the smaller *Ten Jewish American Poets* (1982), and, more recently, the outpouring of works associated with the Jewish feminist movement: *The Tribe of Dina* (1986, rpt. 1989), *Sarah's Daughters Sing* (1990), and individual volumes by poets Alicia Ostriker, Eleanor Wilner, Irena Klepfisz, Charlotte Mandel, Nikki Stiller, Grace Herman and many others. The influences on these poets, both male and female, are undoubtedly many, varied, and complex. Certainly, many found themselves looking for models outside the classrooms, writers who were able to negotiate the language and assumptions of both minority and majority culture. Two influences which I suggest are seminal (though not, of course, in every poet's case) are those, obviously, of Allen Ginsberg, and, less obviously, Sylvia Plath. In their very different approaches to using personal (and Jewish) elements in their work, these poets could be called the father and mother—or the midwives—of the contemporary Jewish American poetry *movement.* Certainly, they each demonstrated ways a Jewish poet might use, revise, and re-imagine his own experiences, both personal and communal, in his verse.

Allen Ginsberg has underplayed or *even* denied the importance of his background, stating, "I don't see myself as a Jew and I am a Jew, and so don't identify with Nation of Jews any more than I would Nation of America or Russia" (Schumacher, 540). Nevertheless, his work is deeply connected to his culture. Eberhart, in the article quoted *above*, described *Howl* as "profoundly Jewish in temper" (Schumacher, 234). It is also structured on Biblical rhythms, as well as on the metrics of William Blake and Christopher Smart. Further, Ginsberg's commitment to absolute honesty in his work—an honesty symbolized by the concept of nakedness, which in his case has sometimes been literal as well as metaphoric—has led him to depict, in many poems, his family's and his own negotiations between being "Jewish" and "American." His readers' enthusiastic responses to this openness underscore the point that for Ginsberg the universal is reached through concentration of the particular—a fact of which the poet is well aware. Speaking of his poem "America," Ginsberg describes it as "an unsystematic and rather gay exposition of my own private beliefs contrary to the official dogmas, but really rather universal, as far as private opinions about which I mention. It says, 'I am thus and so I *have* a right to do so, and I'm saying it out loud for all to hear'" (Schumacher, 219).

Similarly, of his masterwork, *Kaddish*, which brings his Jewish family into the center of his art, Ginsberg says, "I realized it would seem odd to others, but family odd, that is to say familiar-everybody had crazy cousins and aunts and brothers" (Schumacher, 301). In a sense, *Kaddish* is a deconstruction of the well-known American immigrant narrative. In Ginsberg's retelling of this archetypal myth, America drives its newest arrivals mad; all the usual support systems and beliefs—politics, culture, family relationships—break down. The three "sane" family members must finally abandon the non-assimilable mother, who rejects all roles, familial and familiar.

The "Ginsberg" family evoked in the poem is not "universal"; it is recognizably Jewish, and first-generation immigrant American. Its characters are recognizable to many readers, not from literature, but from our lives: the patient, "cultured" father, the earnest, self-denying law-student brother, the intelligent, confused child, and the extravagant, terrified mother with her various attempts to make sense of her world: Communism, nudism, delusions of persecution, fantasies of making lentil soup for an appreciative bachelor God (though unable to satisfy her sons' hungers). The baffled tenderness, guilt and sense of loss that suffuses this poem is surely our own.

142

In a sense, *Kaddish* can be read as a response to all those elders warning their children, "Don't say too much. Don't shame us in front of the goyim, the dominant culture." Ignoring this advice, Ginsberg spills all the family beans, reveals every secret: madness, hallucinations, radical politics, incestuous impulses, homosexuality (his own). In doing so, he creates a painfully great poem, one in which we meet echoes of our own families, with their different, but not all that different, demands on our overwhelming culture.

Young Jewish poets learned at least two things from *Kaddish* (and Ginsberg's work in general): first, that confronting their own lives was acceptable in poetry, was poetry, that the universal can be approached through the particular, and, second, that one's cultural texts, one's sacred literature—one's rhythms—can be reworked to serve personal and aesthetic needs. For *Kaddish* really is a kaddish, a mourner's prayer, an offering in lieu of the traditional prayer that could not be said at Naomi Ginsberg's actual funeral, as there was no minyan, or quorum, of (male) mourners present. Having asked a friend to recite the traditional kaddish, Ginsberg wrote his poem replicating its rhythms, though broken up in manner which suggests sobs (Schumacher, 299-300). Words from the prayer are interjected into the text at crucial points. In the last image of the poem, the speaker's repeated cries of "Lord" are alternated with the "Caws" of crows flying over the graveyard, a stunning verbal and visual metaphor for both the traditional and revisionist impulses of the poem.

While Ginsberg's influence is vast and various, the following poem by David Gershator demonstrates how one Jewish American poet responded to his work:

> Soon it will be April
> the last April
> the first April
> and there will be doors and doors
> and children eager to open them

and a child will go to the door
for the first time
and open it
not knowing what to expect...

In Vilna
I open the door for Elijah
and Elijah comes in and collapses
his once glorious white beard burned off
his angelic face charred beyond belief
He was my grandfather

In Brooklyn
my father commands
Open the door for Elijah
but be careful. First
look through the peephole
There are so many muggers out there
you never know....

(from "Seder")

Sylvia Plath's influence is different. The poems in *Ariel,* were
written only a few years after the triumphant introduction of
Howl to the Bay Area poetry scene, yet was not influenced by
it, or the movement it inspired. Plath, a good student and
well-mannered young poet of her time, had rejected the "self-
pity, self-advertisement, and self-indulgence of the beatniks"
(Alvarez, 25). Yet she felt something was missing in her own
early work; her first book of well-crafted poems, *The Colossus,*
she claimed, now bored her (Alvarez, 24). For her, Robert
Lowell's *Life Studies* was a revelation:

> I've been very excited by what I feel is the new
> breakthrough that came with, say, Robert Lowell's
> Life Studies. This intense breakthrough into very se-
> rious, very personal emotional experience, which...
> has been partly taboo. (Alvarez, 23)

Following Lowell's example (and that of Anne Sexton, whom she met in Lowell's poetry class), Plath was soon writing so-called "confessional" poems. Her work is often praised and damned for the boldness of its revelations—or the intensity of her emotions—concerning events in her own life. "Daddy," for example, is usually seen as a simple wail of rage against Plath's father, Otto Plath, a stubborn man, a German from the Polish Corridor, who kept bees, taught college biology, and died prematurely, the result of an inaccurate self-diagnosis. Depicted in the poem as a Nazi, a devil ("the black man") and a vampire who dies with a "stake in (his) fat, black heart," "Daddy" is the object of the speaker's anger and love. Depending on the reader, her fury can seem liberatory or excessive. Many women readers were impressed with the sheer boldness of this emotion, especially since such anger was not expected (or accepted) from a woman poet. As Ostriker says, "*Ariel...* gave many readers their first taste of unapologetic anger in a woman's poem" (78). Janet Malcolm, who is less sympathetic to Plath, acidly agrees: "Women honor her for her courage to be unpleasant" (95). Other readers have found her anger repellent or even inappropriate. Irving Howe, for example, is disturbed by her use of Holocaust imagery: "There is something monstrous, utterly disproportionate, when tangled emotions about one's father are deliberately compared with the historical fate of the European Jews" (Malcolm, 109). Even George Steiner, who admires Plath's work—with reservations—draws a contrast between the "real" Holocaust and Plath's *ovm* life as "a child, plump and golden in America, when the trains actually went" (Malcolm, 109).

I suggest that, even if "Daddy" and other poems using similar imagery were solely and unambiguously about Plath's own life, such usage would not be inappropriate—especially not in the work of a first-generation German-American poet, trying to understand the implications of World War II and the Holocaust. However, Plath herself has suggested another way in which "Daddy," at least, might be read. According to her

BBC notes, this poem is not autobiographical, but a fictional narrative; the speaker is a "girl" whose father was literally a member of the National Socialist Party in Germany, while her mother was "very possibly part Jewish." This character "has to act out the awful little allegory" implicit in her heritage "before she is free of it" (Ostriker, 102).

While it is hard to disagree with Ostriker, who sees this disclaimer as a rather obvious attempt on Plath's part to distance herself from her emotions (102), let us for the moment take the poet at her word. Certainly, Plath has employed fictitious characters in other poems— "Medusa," "Perseus, or The Triumph of Wit Over Suffering" —figures she has transformed to meet her psychic or aesthetic needs. Let us assume, then, that Plath, in "Daddy," has constructed a fiction involving a protagonist whose identity is both confused and marginalized. The product of a German father and part-Jewish mother in Nazi Germany, she has a problem locating her identity both in the family and in the wider political context. In this poem, power at first seems neatly divided along gender lines: males (Daddy, and the vampire husband-figure) possess it, females (the childlike speaker, the absent "possibly" Jewish mother) do not, though they may "adore" the concept—and the men who wield it. Men, too, are seemingly sure of their identities: Daddy is forthrightly described as part of a distinct (and self-proclaimed predominant) ethnic group. Unlike the speaker, he has command of the German language, an "Aryan eye, bright blue," and a "neat moustache," like his political leader's. The speaker is less sure who she is. She "may be a bit of a Jew"—but then again, she may not. She has trouble speaking German, but has begun "to talk like a Jew." (What a Jew "talks like" is never made clear.) Furthermore, she informs us, she has a "gypsy ancestress" (another marginalized woman), and thus is doubly removed from "Daddy's" Aryan certainties. Daddy is also identified with certain geographical and cultural clues—"the snows of the Tyrol, the clear beer of Vienna" which help to define him. He even has the weapons and symbols of a military culture at his disposal:

he is a "panzer man" with a "Luftwaffe" and a swastika which crowds out the sky.

"Daddy" seems to hold all the cards—but does he? The Tyrolean snows, the Viennese beer, we are told, "are not very pure or true." And the speaker, we learn, has her own, less defined, artifacts and weapons: "weird luck," a "Taroc pack" (this item is repeated, as if for reassurance—or in proud assertion), the allegiance of "the villagers," who agree with her that "Daddy" should be killed. At the poem's end, we see an eerie reversal: the victim-daughter exulting over the death of the powerful father. The marginalized speaker can now marginalize her father, by naming him "bastard," and proclaims herself unable to escape his domination ("I'm through").

While the autobiographical element in this poem cannot be denied, suggest that Plath is not simply telling her own story, but rather using Nazi and Jewish characters and imagery to explore the dynamics of gender, ethnic (racial) and family relationships in a political (or highly politicized) context. For Jewish readers, I think, there were two important implications in her work. While some of us may have agreed with Howe (as I did initially), and others (such as Irena Klepfisz) certainly needed no example from a gentile poet to examine the Holocaust in our poetry, others, as Steiner suggests, were encouraged by her work to think about the issue of the Holocaust as a subject in our art—or conversely, about art as a valid, if not the only, way of trying to grapple with this event. Second, her imaginative identification with Jewish subjects inspired some of us to look more deeply into our own experience.

I suggest that Plath's appeal for many readers is not the fact that she is angry, but because she puts that anger to good use. A poem like "Daddy" can be read as an attempt to reclaim territory, to interject a marginalized speaker—Jewish, gypsy, female, child-into a landscape controlled by a powerful, racially and culturally conquering male figure. In Jewish terms,

Plath may be said to be constructing a "midrash" or imaginative re-interpretation, of issues raised by the holocaust, issues about power relationships in a family and in a society. Certainly for many Jewish poets, especially her work enabled us to enter our own experiences.

The following excerpts from an early Erica Jong poem are an example of this enabling. I strongly suggest that, without the example of Plath's work, this poem could not have been written:

> Europe is dusty plush,
> first-class carriages
> with first-class dust.
> And the conductor
> resembles a pink
> marzipan pig
> and goose steps
> down the corridor.
> FRAULEIN!
> He says it with four umlauts
> My hair's as Aryan
> as anything
> My name is heather.
> My passport, eyes
> bluer than Bavarian skies.
> But he can see
> the Star of David
> in my navel.
> Bump. Grind.
> I wear it for
> the last striptease.
> FRAULEIN!...
> Crisply he notches
> my ticket, then
> his dumpling face smiles down
> in sunlight, which IS

suddenly benign
as chicken soup.

("The 8:29 to Frankfurt")

Here, we can see Jong working her way through Plath's territory, her signature imagery—Aryan hair, "eyes/bluer than Bavarian skies," "the last strip tease" (see "Lady Lazarus") to break through, at the end, to her own: "sunlight/ benign/ as chicken soup." In a sense, this poem can be seen as a paradigm of the process by which many Jewish American poets learned from the "Jewish" poems of Plath and of Ginsberg how they could use their own cultural experiences in their work.

Works Cited

Alvarez, A. *The Savage God: A Study of Suicide.* New York: Random House, 1970.

Gershator, David. "Seder." *Elijah's Child.* Merrick, NY: Cross Cultural Communications, 1992, 27-34.

Ginsberg, Allen. *Kaddish and Other Poems.* San Francisco: City Lights Books, 1961.

Jong, Erica. "The 8:29 to Frankfurt." *Fear of Flying.* New York, Holt, Rhinehart and Winston, 1973, 57-58.

Malcolm, Janet. "The Silent Woman." *The New Yorker.* August 23rd and 30, 1993, pp. 84-97, 100-125, 128-159.

Ostriker, Alicia. *Stealing the Language: the Emergence of Women's Poetry in America.* Boston: Beacon Press, 1986.

Plath, Sylvia. *Collected Poems.* Ed. Ted Hughes. New York: Harper and Row, 19131.

Rich, Adrienne. *What Is Found There: Notebooks on Poetry and Politics.* New York: W.W. Norton, 1993.

Schumacher, Michael. *Dharma Lion: a Critical Biography of Allen Ginsberg.* New York: St. Martin's Press, 1992.

Schwartz, Howard and Anthony Rudolf. *Voices Within the Ark: the Modern Jewish Poets.* New York, Avon, 1980.

Art as Midrash: Some Notes on the Way to a Discussion by Enid Dame

I'm a poet: many of my poems are dramatic monologues, in which characters from Jewish mythology (particularly women) explain or reinterpret their experiences, often from a modem sensibility. In the past, I've called these poems "confessions," but they are in fact midrashim.

If a midrash is a way of filling in gaps left in a text, then much of my art is indeed midrashic. For there were many gaps in my Jewish education. I grew up in a small milltown near Pittsburgh. Most people in my neighborhood were not Jewish. At first, I was the only Jewish child in my grade school. My parents were secular Jews, freethinkers, former radicals and union activists—you get the picture. However, they were still connected to their Jewish upbringings in various ways. They transmitted bits of these pasts, which they obviously found sustaining, on to me. I never received a complete picture, though, which is perhaps why I turned to poems and stories to do the job.

My father's connection was to organized Judaism. He volunteered to teach Sunday School in the Beaver Falls reform temple. In his fifth grade class, he told me, he reconciled the Theory of Evolution with the Creation story in Genesis, his own midrash. One day, he took me with him to a service in a more traditional synagogue, somewhere in the Pennsylvania mountains. It was Simhat Torah, but he didn't tell me that. There was something impressive and mysterious about the event. We walked around and around the room with other people, grown ups and children, following two rabbis carrying marvelous, richly-covered Torahs. We were part of a community, a community of strangers. I knew we were all Jews. Other than that, I didn't know why we were there, but I liked the sense of mystery and feeling of community. (Maybe for my father the sense of community was the religious experience.) I asked my father when we would be given food. "Don't be silly," he said, "This isn't a restaurant." But then the people in charge passed out bags of nuts, apples, and Hershey bars. So the experience was nourishing as well as mysterious and communal.

My mother was uninterested in organized observances. But she gave me a perfect example of a midrash in her reaction to the Genesis story. She took Eve's side and was quite indignant about the matter. "How come everyone blames Eve for what Adam did?" she asked. "After all, he was a grown man. She didn't pry his mouth open and force the fruit in. He was irresponsible, doing what he wanted and letting his wife take the blame!" The implication, louder than speech, was that women often do take the rap for male inadequacies.

From this, I learned that the body of Jewish stories and learning was alive. Myth could excite, and irritate; its characters spoke to us as men and women: we could take sides, comment, reinvent, and thus examine our own lives.

And that's exactly what I do in my "Jewish" poems. Each one is an attempt to understand the world, reach out to it, and (at least through speculation) reconstruct it. To answer those 'persistent, unoriginal questions: how can I exist sanely in this confusing world? In a non-Jewish world, how do I live as a Jew? As a nontraditional Jew, how do I live in relation to other Jews? As a woman, how do I live in a world that allows me no power? (Yes, I know this is supposedly changing.)

Though I write on "non-Jewish" subjects too, my reaction to Jewish material has produced some of my strongest, because most deeply felt, poetry. My poems never start from intellectual decisions. My best poems are often fusions between mythic material and my own concerns, obsessions, etc. A pivotal poem for me (and an interesting one in the light of this conference) is "Vildeh Chaya." Not exactly a midrash, since there is no such character as Vildeh Chaya in Jewish text. I invented her, a wild Jewish woman, because of a misunderstanding on the part of my mother. She thought this Yiddish expression actually referred to an archetypal shtetl character, wild Chaya. So I wrote a poem imagining this character in three incarnations:

1.
Vildeh Chaya
in the woods   on the edge
of the shtetl   she hides
mud splattered   dress torn
barefoot   she won't
peel potatoes   get married
cut her hair off   have children
keep the milk dishes
separate
from the meat dishes.

Instead, she
climbs trees   talks to animals
naked   sings half crazy
songs to the moon.

2.
Vildeh Chaya
in New York
in the sexual 'sixties
lives in a tenement
toilet in hall
wallposters   cats dirty sheets
learns to say "Fuck"
sleeps with men   she meets
at peace demonstrations

later, she
cuts off her hair
sleeps with women
writes poetry.

3.

Vildeh Chaya
in the suburbs   lives alone
on Social Security
afraid of
her floor-length drapes
her glass-topped tables
the color television

her daughter's married
an Orthodox Jew
her son's hitch-hiked
off the edge of the world

she hides when
the mailman knocks
keeps missing
her hairdresser appointments

at night she creeps
around the development
avoiding swimming pools,
the glare of headlights

she's starting
to worry
she's starting to
like her smells.

The idea of this rebellious, quirky, searching Jewish woman appealed to me. "Vildeh Chaya" expressed something deep in my own psyche and imagination. But then I realized she already existed in Jewish mythology. She was Lilith, Adam's first wife, the first feminist, the woman who voluntarily walked out on Eden.

I found this character courageous, touching and funny. It was especially significant that she is not simply portrayed as

reckless or outrageous. She is intelligent (arguing logically
with Adam): she is sure of herself sexually. The freedom she
chooses is not easy or painless.

True, wild, defiant or questioning women appear in other
traditions; think of Kali, think of Antigone, and I like those
women too. But there was something special for me in the
idea of Lilith as a Jewish archetype. In a sense, discovering
her was liberating for me; the fact of her existence in myth
suggested possibilities for female strength and independence
within the Jewish tradition. Of course, the patriarchs consider
Lilith a demon (they would!); true, she represents male fear
of women, or of their own sexuality. But she also represents
the possibility of defining oneself on one's own terms, as a
woman and a Jew. She helped me widen my expectations.
My first Lilith poem was too angry, too ideological, simply
a "party line" feminist poem. I discarded it. The second, or
first authentic, Lilith poem was written out of a wrenching
personal experience. Put simply, I had chosen to leave a mar-
riage and all that the marriage represented for a totally dif-
ferent, less certain life. I had, for a long time, retained a fan-
tasy that I could go back to the old circumstances, if I wished.
The day I realized I couldn't, that I had consciously set the
process in motion that made returning impossible, that was
the day 1 wrote "Lilith." The images poured out; it needed
almost no revision.

           kicked myself out of paradise
           left a hole in the morning
           no note   no goodbye

           the man I lived with
           was patient and hairy

           he cared for the animals
           worked late at night
           planting vegetables
           under the moon

sometimes he'd hold me
our long hair tangled
he kept me from rolling
off the planet

it was
always safe there
but safety

wasn't enough.   I kept nagging
pointing out flaws
in his logic

he carried a god
around in his pocket
consulted it like
a watch or an almanac

it always proved
I was wrong

two against one isn't fair! I cried
and stormed out of Eden
into history

the middle ages
were sort of fun
they called me a witch
I kept dropping
in and out
of people's sexual fantasies

Now
I work in New Jersey
take art lessons
live with a cab driver

he says: baby
what I like about you
is your sense of humor

sometimes
I cry in the bathroom
remembering Eden
and the man and the god
I couldn't live with.

Let's move to a completely different Jewish woman, Lot's
Wife. What interested me here was not her act of rebellion
(looking back on Sodom) but her numbness, her survival.
(Friends tell me they've seen her recently, a rock on an Israe-
li desert.) Is numbness a metaphor? I wondered. Do women
numb themselves as a way of coping, of managing to remain
unhurt? Did my mother do this? Do I? Is this a female re-
sponse to a puzzling, demeaning, often violent world? Mrs.
Lot survives marriage, loss of children, exile, holocaust of
her city, but at the price of being a permanent statue. In a
way, she's heroic, though crippled.

(Lot's Wife)

I'm not surprised
this happened   in some ways
I
was always numb

standing before the stove
braiding my daughters' hair

numb as a rock
in the ritual bath

hard to raise daughters
in that city
where men loved each other

or
entertained angels

always suspected
movement
was dangerous

they called him the most righteous man
in Sodom   in bed
I'd feel him
knocking against me
like someone opening
a window
in another room

now I don't feel
anything at all.
It isn't so different.

Let me conclude with a midrash on a male character—Lot. What interested me about him was the fact that he found himself in a situation where no rules applied. Being a Jew, being Abraham's nephew didn't help. His city was destroyed, his marriage dissolved, even the incest taboos were suspended for him. His conclusion might well have been: Don't believe this officially, I still want to believe that we can change the world for the better – I sometimes suspect he may be right.

(Lot)

When I first knew the world
things were simple:
tables   chairs   bottles
stayed within outlines,
held no surprises.

Uncle Abraham said
there's a pattern to things:

pull off your foreskin,
God's happy;
turn away guests,
he's outraged.
On Uncle's earth, laws
grasped each stone,
each struck match   or raised knife.
For years, I lived there.

Then the world wrenched
half off its stalk.
Windows slammed down.

Sky
crushed to an ocean of heat
fell on us, melting
houseguests to angels,

city to garbagedump,
wife to a block of rock salt
and daughters to wives.

When she crawled over me
first, all I felt
were elbows and knobs:
rock sliding on rock
in our cave

then, the rock softened
and flowed.

My two sons grow fat,
call me "Grandpa."
I could lie to myself.
(Wine takes the sting out of memory.)
Still, what's the point?
People who don't live in caves
think they know everything   visit us

like to pretend they're shocked.
(Maybe they really are shocked.)

They say they've got answers.
Answers
swarm round their heads, angry bees.
They'd never ask questions.

Sometimes,
they point to us,
say, "This is crazy."

Sometimes
I point to God,
say, "This is crazy."

God says,
"I know."

Appendix 4

a selected list of Enid Dame's publications

AN ENID DAME BIBLIOGRAPHY

Anything You Don't See
West End Press, 1992.
ISBN 0-931122-67-8

Between Revolutions
Downtown Poets Co-op, 1977.
ISBN 0-917402-02-2

Confessions
Cross-Cultural Communications, 1982.
ISBN 0-89304-811-9

Interesting Times
Downtown Poets Co-op, 1978.
ISBN 0-917402-09-X

Lilith and Her Demons
Cross-Cultural Communications, 1986.
ISBN 0-89304-408-3

On the Road to Damascus, Maryland
Downtown Poets, 1980.
ISBN 0-917402-15-4

Stone Shekhina
Three Mile Harbor, 2002.
ISBN 1-886124-02-10

Which Lilith? Feminist Writers Re-Create the World's First Woman. Jason Aronson, 1998. (Co-edited with Lilly Rivlin and Henny Wenkart).
ISBN 0-7657-6015-0

Published posthumously:

A mythic country she never quite believed in—Poems touching on the Israeli/Palestinian Conflict.
Bard Press/Ten Penny Players, 2008.
ISBN 0-934776-13-X

Where is the Woman?—Letters and Poems from California
Shivastan Publishing, Woodstock, NY, 2006.
(A memorial volume in a limited edition craft printed in Kathmandu, Nepal).

Contributor Notes

Laurence Carr writes fiction, poetry and for the theatre. His book of microfiction, *The Wytheport Tales*, is published by Codhill Press, and he is the editor of *Riverine: An Anthology of Hudson Valley Writers* and co-editor of *WaterWrites: A Hudson River Anthology*, also from Codhill. His prose and poetry have been seen in publications such as *Home Planet News*, *Chronogram*, and *Out of Line*. Over 25 of his plays and theatre pieces have been produced in NYC, regionally and abroad in Warsaw, Prague, and Bratislava. Laurence teaches Dramatic and Creative Writing at SUNY New Paltz where he runs the SUNY Playwrights' Project and co-edits *Stonesthrow Review*.

Patricia Eakins is the author of *The Hungry Girls and Other Stories* and *The Marvelous Adventures of Pierre Baptiste* (a novel) which won the NYU Press Prize for Fiction and the Capricorn Fiction Award of the Writer's Voice. Her work has appeared in *The Iowa Review, Parnassus, Conjunctions*, and *The Paris Review*, which awarded her the Aga Khan Prize. Eakins has also been awarded two fellowships from the National Endowment for the Arts and the Charles Angoff Award from *The Literary Review*. Françoise Palleau's French translation of *The Hungry Girls* is forthcoming from the University of Grenoble Press. Eakins curates the Sunday Best Reading Series in Northern Manhattan.

David Gershator taught Humanities at Rutgers, Brooklyn College, CUNY, and the University of the Virgin Islands. He is a recipient of an NEH grant and a NY State CAPS award. David has published translations, poetry, and reviews in numerous anthologies and journals. He was co-editor of *Downtown Poets Co-op* and an Associate Editor at *Home Planet News*. He is the translator and editor of *Federico García Lorca: Selected Letters*. David also co-authored six picture books and a music CD for children. His poetry books include *Play Mas* and *Elijah's Child*.

Phillis Gershator has worked as an academic, public, and a school librarian, and is the author of a reference book, a poetry chapbook, and two dozen books for children for which she has received several awards. She also co-edited *Downtown Poets*, a small press poetry publisher in NY. Her poetry, articles, and reviews have appeared in journals such as *The Caribbean Writer* and *Home Planet News*. She has poetry in several anthologies for adults, and stories and poems for children in *Highlights* and *The Cricket Group* magazines. Phillis lives with her husband and frequent co-author, David Gershator, in the U.S. Virgin Islands.

Roberta Gould, whose work has appeared in many poetry journals, is the author of eight poetry collections, including *Writing Air, Written Water, Only Rock, Not By Blood Alone, Esta Naranja, Pacing the Wind,* and her latest, *Louder than Seeds* (FootHills Publishing). She organized an awareness campaign to debunk the price haggling myth and to teach Europeans that tipping is a necessity when they travel in Latin America.

Walter Hess was born in Germany in 1931 and emigrated with his family to the US in 1940, via Ecuador. He was educated in New York City Schools with a BA from CCNY in 1952 and an MA from CCNY in 2003. He is a retired documentary film editor. Films on which he collaborated have won numerous awards, including two Peabody's and three Emmy's. Metamorphoses has published his translations from the German of the poetry of Hans Sahl. A book of poetry, *Jew's Harp*, will appear in 2010.

Bob Holman, founder and proprietor of the Bowery Poetry Club, is a poet most often connected with spoken word, performance, hiphop and slam. He has published nine books of poetry and released two CDs. His latest collection of poems, a collaboration with Chuck Close, is *A Couple of Ways of Doing Something* (Aperture). His most recent CD is "The Awesome Whatever" (Bowery Books). The TV series he produced for PBS, "The United States of Poetry," won the INPUT (International Public Television) Award; he founded Mouth Almighty/Mercury Records, the first ever major spoken word label; and founded and ran the infamous poetry slams at the Nuyorican Poets Café, where he also co-edited the American Book Award-winning anthology, *Aloud!*. His major project these days is a documentary series on the Poetry of Endangered Languages, with recent trips to West Africa, India and Israel/Palestine.

Dimitrios Kalantzis was born and raised in Sheepshead Bay, Brooklyn. In 2005, he moved to Chicago, Illinois, where he is completing a Master's degree in journalism. His work appears in a number of different print and online news sites.

Burt Kimmelman has published six collections of poetry; *Musaics* (Sputyen Duyvil Press, 1992), *First Life* (Jensen/Daniels Publishing, 2000), *The Pond at Cape May Point* (Marsh Hawk Press, 2002), a collaboration with the painter Fred Caruso, *Somehow* (Marsh Hawk Press, 2005), *There Are Words* (Dos Madres Press, 2007), and *As If Free* (Talisman House, Publishers, 2009). For over a decade he was Senior Editor of *Poetry New York: A Journal of Poetry and Translation*.

He is a professor of English at New Jersey Institute of Technology and the author of two book-length literary studies: *The "Winter Mind": William Bronk and American Letters* (Fairleigh Dickinson University Press, 1998); and *The Poetics of Authorship in the Later Middle Ages: The Emergence of the Modern Literary Persona* (Peter Lang Publishing, 1996; paperback 1999). He also edited *The Facts on File Companion to 20th-Century American Poetry* (Facts on File, 2005) and co-edited *The Facts on File Companion to American Poetry* (2007). He has published scores of essays on medieval, modern, and contemporary poetry.

Careufel de Lamière was born via mid-wife in August 1940 in Plainville, CT on the chicken farm of her paternal grandfather, Authur Dame. She won AFWL short story prizes in USAF (Ohio, Libya) and studied with Dr. Leonie Adams, Robert Burtt, Eve Merriam, Irwin Stark, Anatole Broyard and C.D.B. Bryan. Her first completed novel, *With None Beside,* has not been published and first completed play, "A Great Thud of Water," never produced. She earned a B.A. and an M.A. from CCNY in 1970 and 1976. As Robin Lamiere, she did collages and photos for Enid Dame's first two books of poetry. Careufel joined *Home Planet News* at its inception as Fiction Editor; at present, she is co-Executive Editor under her legal name of Careufel de Lamière.

Judith Lechner has had her poetry published in *Chronogram, Home Planet News, Jews, Country and Abroad* and other publications and in anthologies *Be Mine; Green Heron Poets* (Narrowsburg, NY), *25* (Arts Society of Kingston, NY) and *Wildflowers* (Shivistan Pub). Her poems and essays have been read on radio (WAMC, WKZE, WDST) and interpreted with visual art at Alliance Gallery and Arts Society of Kingston. She has read extensively throughout the

Hudson Valley. Currently she is working on memoir, short stories, and a play.

Linda Lerner is the author of thirteen poetry collections, the most recent from Iniquity Press / Vendetta books, *Something Is Burning in Brooklyn*, (2009), *Living in Dangerous Times* (Presa Press, 2007) and *City Woman* (March Street Press, 2006). The last two collections were *Small Press Reviews'* Pick of the Month. Her poems have recently appeared in—or are forthcoming from—*The Literary Gazette*, *The New York Quarterly*, *BigCityLit*, *Home Planet News*, *Big Hammer*, *Mobius*, and *Chiron Review*.

Donald Lev was born in New York City in 1936. He attended Hunter College, worked in the wire rooms of both the *Daily News* and *New York Times*, and then drove a taxi cab for twenty years (with a six year hiatus in which he ran messages for and contributed poetry to *The Village Voice* and operated the Home Planet Bookshop on the Lower East Side). His earliest poems appeared in print in 1958, and he started his first small press magazine, *HYN Anthology*, in 1969, the same year his brief underground film acting career pinnacled with his portrayal (he wrote his own lines) of the Poet in Robert Downey Sr.'s classic *Putney Swope*. He met Enid Dame (1943-2003) at a N.Y. Poet's Co-operative meeting in 1976. They became life partners in 1978, and in 1979 founded the literary tabloid *Home Planet News*, which Lev still publishes.

Ellen (Aug) Lytle teaches creative writing at Bronx Community College, won a poetry prize in 2006 from Columbia, is working towards a book of selected poems, knew and liked Enid Dame, the person and the poet, so very much, is an animal welfare activist, loves painting, peanuts and her giant family.

Patricia Markert was born and grew up in Syracuse, New York. While she was an undergraduate at the University of Iowa, she edited *Me Too,* a literary magazine, with Mary Swanson. Since moving to New York City, she has worked in the publishing industry and is now a librarian. Her poetry has appeared in *American Poetry Review, St. Luke's Review* and *Home Planet News,* and in her chapbook, *Watched You Disappear.*

D. H. Melhem's eight books of poetry include *Art and Politics / Politics and Art* (2010), *New York Poems* (2005), *Conversation with a Stonemason* (2003), Country (1998), and *Rest in Love* (1975, 1978, 1995). She has published a trilogy of novels (*Blight,* optioned as a feature film, *Stigma and The Cave*). Other works include two critical studies of Black poets, a musical drama, a creative writing workbook, over 70 essays, and two anthologies. Among awards for poetry and prose: an American Book Award, a National Endowment for the Humanities Fellowship, and a RAWI Lifetime Achievement Award (2007). She serves as vice-president of the International Women's Writing Guild.

Constance Norgren is the author of the chapbook *Same Boat* and co-author (with Lois Adams, Barbara Elovic and Patricia Markert) of *To Genesis,* both from 5 Spice Press. *To Genesis* was inspired by their work with Enid Dame and contains an introduction by Enid. Norgren has had poems published in *West Branch, Heliotrope,* and *Yankee,* as well as in other journals. She has been a teacher of young children for over thirty years and lives with her family in Brooklyn, New York.

Alicia Ostriker is a poet and midrashist, author of *The Nakedness of the Fathers: Biblical Visions and Revisions* and *The Volcano Sequence.*

Cheryl A. Rice's poetry has appeared in *Art Times*, *The Baltimore Review*, *Chronogram*, *The Florida Review*, *Home Planet News*, *Mangrove*, *Poetry Motel*, *Poets Gallery Press*, *The Temple/El Templo*, and *The Woodstock Times*, and online at albanypoets.com, poetrypoetry.com, and thehiddencity.com. She has made New York's Hudson Valley her home for almost 30 years. She holds a B.S. from the State University of New York, College at New Paltz, and studied English at the University at Albany. She has also studied poetry with Maria Mazziotti Gillan, Enid Dame, Joan Murray and former NYS Poet Laureate Sharon Olds.

Edward Sanders is a poet, historian and musician. His selected poems, *1986-2008, Let's Not Keep Fighting the Trojan War*, has been published by Coffee House Press. Another recent writing project is *Poems for New Orleans*, a book and CD on the history of that great city, and its tribulations during and after hurricane Katrina. Other books in print include *Tales of Beatnik Glory* (4 volumes published in a single edition), *1968, a History in Verse*, *The Poetry and Life of Allen Ginsberg*, *The Family*, a history of the Charles Manson murder group, and *Chekhov*, a biography in verse of Anton Chekhov. Sanders was the founder of the satiric folk/rock group, The Fugs, which has released many albums and CDs during its 45 year history. He lives in Woodstock, New York with his wife, the essayist and painter Miriam Sanders, and both are active in environmental and other social issues.

Judith Saunders is Professor of English at Marist College, where she teaches American literature and creative writing, including courses focusing on contemporary poetry and Hudson River Valley literature. In addition to scholarly commentary on figures such as Henry David Thoreau, Edith Wharton, Gwendolyn Brooks, Elizabeth Bishop, Charles Tomlinson, and others, she has published poetry, creative nonfiction, and humor for general audiences. Her work has appeared in regional literary magazines such as *The Art Times, The Hudson River Valley Review, Home Planet News,* and *Chronogram,* as well as in national publications such as *The North American Review, California Quarterly, Bay Windows, Poetry Miscellany,* and *The Journal of Irreproducible Results.*

Susan Sindall's poems have appeared in *The Kenyon Review, Prairie Schooner, Salamander, The Seattle Review,* and *Pivot,* among other journals. She's been awarded fellowships by The MacDowell Colony, Ragdale, and The Virginia Center for the Performing Arts and is a graduate of The Warren Wilson MFA for Writers. Her book, *What's Left,* was just recently released by Cherry Grove Collections.

Harry Smith is a poet, editor and essayist who now lives in Maine. Smith first became known in the small press world as the editor of *The Smith,* a literary magazine and small press founded in the mid-1960s. Topical prose can be found in *The Sexy Sixties* (2002), poetry in *Trinity* (1975), *Sonnets to P.L.A.* (1979), and *Ballads for the Possessed* (1987). His magazine and press featured among others James T. Farrell, Menke Katz, Stanley Nelson, Sidney Bernard, Bill Rane and Richard (Ward) Morris. A new anthology of avant-garde poetry *Inside the Outside* (2006) features a generous selection of his poetry. He is married to the playwright Clare Melley Smith.

Matthew J. Spireng's full-length book manuscript *Out of Body* won the 2004 Bluestem Poetry Award and was published in 2006 by Bluestem Press at Emporia State University. His chapbooks are: *Young Farmer, Encounters, Inspiration Point*, winner of the 2000 Bright Hill Press Poetry Chapbook Competition; and *Just This*. He lives in Ulster County, New York, which is where he discovered the unique and wonderful voice of Enid Dame.

Nikki Stilller was born in 1947 to a Russian-Jewish bookkeeper and a man with an aversion to work. She holds a Ph.D. from CUNY in English, has published five books and several dozen articles. She lives in New York with her 16 year old son and her new husband. For many years, she was a professor of English at the New Jersey Institute of Technology.

Yerra Sugarman is the author of two poetry collections, both published by The Sheep Meadow Press: *Forms of Gone* (2002) and *The Bag of Broken Glass* (2008). She has received many honors, among them a PEN/Joyce Osterweil Award for Poetry, a "Discovery/The Nation" Poetry Prize, a Canada Council Grant for Creative Writers, a Glenna Luschei Prairie Schooner Award, and awards from the Poetry Society of America. Her poetry, translations and critical writing have appeared in *The Nation, Prairie Schooner, The Massachusetts Review, Literary Imagination, Poetry International,* and *Pleiades,* among other publications. She teaches creative writing at Rutgers University.

Maxine Susman met Enid Dame when they worked together in the Writing Program at Rutgers-New Brunswick in the late '80s. Enid encouraged her to write and published her first poem in *Home Planet News*. Since then Susman's work has appeared in several dozen journals and anthologies, including *Home Planet News, Paterson Literary Review, Ekphrasis, Earth's Daughters, Colere, Dogwood,* and *Poet Lore.*

173

Her chapbooks are *Gogama*, 2006, and two collections in 2009, *Wartime Address* and *Familiar*. Recent poetry awards include Honorable Mention in the Allen Ginsberg, Black River, and Dogwood Journal contests. She is Professor of English at Caldwell College where she has taught poetry, English literature, composition, and honors courses for 10 years, after stints at Rutgers University, Seton Hall, and as a Caldwell exchange professor at Duksung Women's University in Seoul, Korea. She is a member of the poetry performance group Cool Women and lives with her husband Jay Harris in Highland Park, NJ.

Karen Swenson has published five books of poems. The most recent is *A Pilgrim into Silence*. She won the National Poetry Series with her volume, *The Landlady in Bangkok*. Her travel and political articles have been published by *The New York Times*, *The Wall Street Journal*, and *The New Leader*. She has taught at Barnard College, Denver University, Scripps, Clark and Skidmore.

Madeline Tiger's recent collections are *The Earth Which Is All* (2008) and *Birds of Sorrow and Joy: New and Selected Poems, 1970-2000* (2003). Her next collection, *The Atheist's Prayer*, will appear from Dos Madres Press in 2010. Her work appears regularly in journals and anthologies. She has been teaching in state programs and private workshops since 1973 and has been a "Dodge Poet" since 1986. She has five children and seven grandchildren and lives in Bloomfield, NJ under a weeping cherry tree.

Martin Tucker is Editor-in-Chief of the prize-winning literary journal, *Confrontation*. He is the author of four collections of poetry, the most recent, *Plenty of Exits: New and Selected Poems* (2008). His newest book is a study of exile and its aftermaths, *Boundaries of Exile, Conditions of Hope*, which he wrote in collaboration with Albert Russo (Confrontation Press, 2009). Among his other books are the widely-praised *Literary Exile in the Twentieth Century* (Greenwood Press, 1991), *Sam Shepard, Joseph Conrad and Africa in Modern Literature*, the first book published in the U.S. on African Literature. He has edited more than 20 volumes of literary encyclopedia, among them *A Library of Literary Criticism* and *The Critical Temper*. He served on the Executive Board of PEN American Center for 23 years and for two terms on the Governing Board of Poetry Society of America. His essays and reviews have appeared in *The New York Times Book Review, The Nation, The New Republic, The Commonweal, Saturday Review of Literature*, and *Research in African Literatures*. He is Professor Emeritus of Long Island University, where he taught for more than 35 years and served as the Chair of the English Department of the Brooklyn Center of LIU for two terms.

Janine Pommy Vega is the author of eighteen books and chapbooks since 1968. The latest is (poetry) *The Green Piano*, Godine, May 2005. Her first CD, *Across the Table, recorded in Woodstock, and from live performances in Italy and Bosnia*, came out in November, 2007. An Italian translation of her travel book *Tracking the Serpent* (Sulle tracce del serpente, Nutrimenti, Rome) was published in July 2007. Her translations from Spanish of migrant workers' poems, *Estamos Aquí*, came out from Bowery Books in 2007. Vega performs with music and solo, in English and Spanish, in international poetry festivals, museums, prisons, universities, cafes, nightclubs, and migrant workers' camps in South America, North America and Europe. She is the Director of Incisions/Arts, an organization of writers working with people behind bars, and has taught inside prisons for more than twenty-five years. She currently teaches a course in poetics for Bard Prison Initiative.

Carletta Joy Walker, an American-based writer, poet and performer as well as journalist and producer, uses the media and her work in public to encourage communication and respect. Carletta wishes to encourage through her work an appreciation of our stories as essential elements to our well-being. She is the founder of Joy Works Everywhere! Inc, a center in development for learning peaceful and holistic living.

Barry Wallenstein is the author of six collections of poetry, the most recent being *Tony's World* (Birchbrook Press, 2010). His special interest is presenting his poetry in collaboration with jazz. The latest recording, *Euphoria Ripens* (Cadence Jazz Records), was listed among the "Best Jazz Recordings of 2008" in *AllAboutJazz* magazine. He is an Emeritus Professor of literature and creative writing at the City College of New York and an editor of the journal, *American Book Review*. At City, in 1972, he initiated the Annual Spring Poetry Festival which continues to this day. Both Donald Lev and Enid Dame were participants from the beginning.

Acknowledgments

P. 11 —"Some Thoughts on the Life and Work of Enid Dame" by Donald Lev was first published in *Jewish Currents*.

P. 35 —"Enid Dame's Householdry" by Burt Kimmelman appeared in *Rain Taxi*, Summer 2009, Online Edition.

p. 48 —"Remembering Enid" by Careufel de Lamière was first printed in *Home Planet News*, Issue 50, 2004.

p. 52 —"On Enid Dame" by Linda Lerner was first printed in *Small Press Review* (September/October 2004).

P. 59 —"Enid Dame's Legacy, from Enid Dame Tribute, March 21, 2004, Cedar Tavern" by D. H. Melhem first appeared in *Home Planet News*, Issue 53, 2005.

P. 84 —"Bless This Garden, a review of *Stone Shekhina*, Poems by Enid Dame" by Madeline Tiger first appeared in *Bridges*, Volume 10, Number 1, Spring 2004.

P. 99 —"Chagall Exhibit, 1996" by Enid Dame first appeared in *Many Mountains Moving*, Volume 4, Number 1, 1999.

P. 101 —"Mike Gold and the Classics" by Enid Dame first appeared in *Bridges*, Volume 4, Number 1, 1994.

P. 103 —"Lilith, I Don't Cut My Grass" by Enid Dame first appeared in *Stone Shekhina, Poems by Enid Dame* (Three Mile Harbor Press, 2002).

P. 105 —"The Woman Who Was Water" by Enid Dame first appeared in *Nashim: A Journal of Jewish Woman's Studies*, Spring # 19, 2010.

P, 109 —"Russian Snow" by David Gershator first appeared in *Home Planet News*, Issue 45, 1999.

P. 111 —"Poetry Teacher" by Roberta Gould was first published in *Home Planet News,* Issue 53, Fall 2005.

P. 112 —"Bat Mitzvah—Portion Noah" by Walter Hess first appeared in *Jew's Harp* (Pleasure Boat Studio, 2009).

P. 115 —"Enid" by Judith Lechner first appeared in *Home Planet News,* Issue 51, 2004.

P. 117 —"Epithalamion for Enid and Don" by D. H. Melhem first appeared in *Home Planet News,* Issue 50, 2004.

P. 120 —"For Enid Dame" by Ed Sanders was first published in *Home Planet News,* Issue 50, 2004.

P. 123 —"Lilith Mourns" by Matthew J. Spireng was first published in *Heliotrope,* Volume 5, Winter 2004.

P. 131 —"Enid" by Janine Pommy Vega was first published in *Home Planet News,* Issue 50, 2004.

P. 133 —"Sparkle Like Diamonds, A Review" by Carletta Joy Walker first appeared in *Home Planet News,* 2004.

P. 136 —"Without Tears for Enid" by Barry Wallenstein first appeared in *Heliotrope,* Volume 5, Winter 2004.

P. 150 —"Art as Midrash: Some Notes on the Way to a Discussion" by Enid Dame first appeared in *Home Planet News,* Issue 53, Fall 2005.

About NYQ Books™

NYQ Books™ was established in 2009 as an imprint of The New York Quarterly Foundation, Inc. Its mission is to augment the New York Quarterly poetry magazine by providing an additional venue for poets already published in the magazine. A lifelong dream of NYQ's founding editor, William Packard, NYQ Books™ has been made possible by both growing foundation support and new technology that was not available during William Packard's lifetime. We are proud to present these books to you and hope that you will continue to support The New York Quarterly Foundation, Inc. and our poets and that you will enjoy these other titles from NYQ Books™:

Barbara Blatner	*The Still Position*
Amanda J. Bradley	*Hints and Allegations*
rd coleman	*beach tracks*
Joanna Crispi	*Soldier in the Grass*
Ira Joe Fisher	*Songs from an Earlier Century*
Sanford Fraser	*Tourist*
Tony Gloeggler	*The Last Lie*
Ted Jonathan	*Bones & Jokes*
Richard Kostelanetz	*Recircuits*
Iris Lee	*Urban Bird Life*
Kevin Pilkington	*In the Eyes of a Dog*
Jim Reese	*ghost on 3rd*
F. D. Reeve	*The Puzzle Master and Other Poems*
Jackie Sheeler	*Earthquake Came to Harlem*
Jayne Lyn Stahl	*Riding with Destiny*
Norman Stock	*Impunity*
Tim Suermondt	*Just Beautiful*
Douglas Treem	*Everything so Seriously*
Oren Wagner	*Voluptuous Gloom*
Joe Weil	*The Plumber's Apprentice*
Pui Ying Wong	*Yellow Plum Season*
Fred Yannantuono	*A Boilermaker for the Lady*
Grace Zabriskie	*Poems*

Please visit our website for these and other titles:

www.nyqbooks.org

Breinigsville, PA USA
17 December 2010
251567BV00007B/1/P